MW00776766

High Altitude Vegetable Gardening
A Guide to Organic Abundance at Any Elevation

Kevin Korb

HighAltitudeVegetableGardening@gmail.com

Front Cover: "Young Kale" Watercolor by Leanne Korb

Table of Contents

Introduction

When I first moved from sea level up to the mountains at 8,000 feet, I was repeatedly told it was impossible to grow vegetables at such a high elevation. I was given vague arguments about how it was too cold, too dry, there were too many animals, the soil was too poor, and the wind just too destructive. Despite these warnings, I stubbornly set off to start a garden. I quickly found that, yes, in fact, it was cold, it was dry, the wildlife was abundant, the soil wasn't great, and yes, the wind would occasionally blow me over, but I also found all those hindrances could easily be overcome.

Too often people are overwhelmed by the sheer quantity of challenges in front of them, and instead of tackling each one individually, they see them as one insurmountable obstacle. High altitude gardening is not a single insurmountable challenge, but instead a series of smaller, more manageable ones.

When you tease apart the individual factors that affect high altitude gardening, you quickly understand that they are not unique to any location. Almost every gardener, even ones at sea level, will at times be challenged by cold, dry, and windy weather, along with invading critters, and less than ideal soil. What is unique, is that at high altitudes these challenges are more frequent, more intense, and each challenge may even happen all on the same day. It is your ability to see these challenges as separate obstacles and address them individually that can turn a seemingly impossible situation into something altogether more manageable and pleasant.

After all, it is these challenges that make gardening the beautiful hobby that it is. If it weren't for the difficulties, there would be no reward. It is the obstacles we face head on and learn to overcome that make gardening so worthwhile. High altitude gardening is an opportunity to transform some of the wildest land in the world into an oasis of healthy, edible plants. While in a very practical sense, gardening at high altitudes is a series of challenges, it is also a singular great opportunity. And it is not the gardening knowledge we hold, but our willingness to take on that opportunity that makes us great gardeners.

And yet, some knowledge is still necessary. Whether it comes through direct experience or through books, if you don't know what you're doing, your garden will not thrive. Unfortunately, too often the ability to care for plants is viewed as a natural, inherent gift you either have or you don't. People call this having a green thumb, and I very much disagree with the concept. Caring for plants is something we learn. Some people grew up around plants and that is how they learned to care for them. Others weren't so lucky and need a bit more instruction. But a green thumb is not something you do have or don't have, it's something you do have or don't have *yet*. Everyone is capable of being an incredible gardener and every piece of land is capable of becoming an incredible garden.

You don't need to have gardened for thirty years or have a degree in agriculture to have a successful garden in a challenging climate. In this book I've laid out a framework that you can use to create and enjoy your own healthy and productive vegetable garden. And it's really not that hard. The information is simple and straightforward and will help you navigate your garden from planning to harvest.

In part one of this book, we explore what makes your garden plot unique, and from there determine what vegetables will grow best. If you don't understand the specifics of your garden, you will likely find yourself blindsided by challenges that could easily be fixed or avoided. The first step to a successful garden anywhere, but especially at high altitudes, is thoroughly understanding your garden plot, and then using that information to create a realistic and achievable plan.

In part two of the book, we look at solutions to some of the biggest challenges facing high altitude gardeners, including a cold, short growing season, arid climate, strong winds, hungry wildlife, weeds, low pollination, and poor soil, as well as pests and diseases.

Part three is a reference section with the distinct growing parameters of the most common garden vegetables. This section can and should be regularly referred to over the years as you perfect growing food in your unique garden.

Gardening is a truly beautiful endeavor that should not

needlessly be limited by altitude. Whether you're gardening at 5,000 feet or 11,000 feet, use this book and create your own abundant and healthy garden.

Part One

Know Your Garden and Make a Plan

Know Your Garden 1

The first step in creating a healthy and productive garden is understanding everything that makes your garden plot unique. Everywhere, but especially at high altitudes, the individual factors affecting a piece of land can change, not from town to town, or mile to mile, but literally foot to foot. Until you understand your garden and all the factors affecting it, you won't be able to utilize the land's strengths and improve its weaknesses to create your best garden possible.

Your Climate

Some of the factors affecting your climate are the same throughout your entire state, while others may only affect a single plant within your garden. To understand your garden's climate, it is necessary to understand the overarching broad factors, like seasons and weather patterns, as well as the more unique factors that are specific to your garden plot, like shade from a tree or radiant heat from a building.

Hardiness Zones

A great initial tool for gaining a baseline understanding of your garden climate is the USDA Plant Hardiness Zone Map (fig.1). This map gives an estimate of your area's typical wintertime low temperature. This map is a quick and easy way to understand your garden climate and figure out what plants can and can't grow all-year round.

For example, if you live in Zone 10 or colder then you will have a typical wintertime low temperature below 32 degrees, and you shouldn't plant frost intolerant crops that need more than a year to grow, such as artichokes, avocados, and bananas.

Given that most high altitude areas experience severe winters, this zoning information, by itself, may simply confirm what you already know: winter is cold. And while there are some perennial fruits and vegetables that can survive even the most intense winters (table 1), this book focuses mainly on annual vegetables that grow in the spring, summer, and fall.

Fig. 1 USDA Plant Hardiness Zone Map

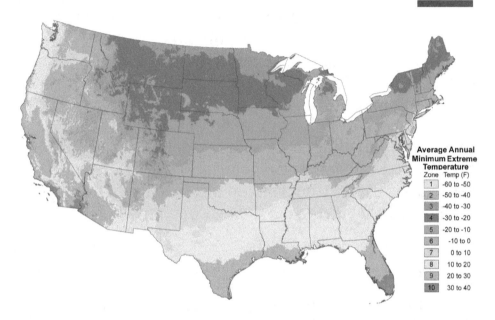

Average Annual Minimum Extreme Temperature

Zone	Temp (F)
1	-60 to -50
2	-50 to -40
3	-40 to -30
4	-30 to -20
5	-20 to -10
6	-10 to 0
7	0 to 10
8	10 to 20
9	20 to 30
10	30 to 40

Last and First Frost Dates

More helpful than simply knowing your hardiness zone, is knowing your estimated last spring and first fall frost dates. These frost dates are frequently used to help determine when to plant your annual vegetables.

For example, since tomatoes will die from even a light frost, by knowing your last spring frost date, you'll know when you can start planting tomatoes outside. Kale, as another example, is happy with a light to moderate frost, but still, if it gets too cold it will die. Therefore, it's recommended that you plant kale no more than 4 weeks before the last spring frost date.

To find your area's frost dates visit: www.plantmaps.com. On this website you will also find great information like monthly precipitation and monthly temperature highs and lows.

Table 1
Perennial High Altitude Fruits and Vegetables

Plant	Hardiness Zone	Sun	Ideal pH
Apples*	3	Full Sun	5.5-6.5
Asparagus	3	Full Sun or Light Shade	6.0-8.0
Blackberries	5-6	Full Sun or Light Shade	5.5-7.0
Blueberries**	4	Full Sun or Light Shade	4.0-5.0
Cherries	4	Full Sun	6.0-6.5
Chives	3	Full Sun or Partial Shade	5.5-7.0
Chokeberries	3-4	Full Sun or Light Shade	6.0-7.0
Currants	3	Full Sun or Partial Shade	5.5-6.5
Elderberries	3	Full Sun or Light Shade	5.5-6.5
Goji Berries	5	Full Sun	6.5-7.0
Gooseberries	3	Light Shade or Partial Shade	6.0-7.0
Horseradish	3	Full Sun or Partial Shade	6.0-7,5
Lavander	5	Full Sun	6.5-7.0
Mahonia Berries	5	Light Shade or Partial Shade	6.0-8.0
Mint	4	Full Sun or Partial Shade	7.0-8.0
Oregano	4	Full Sun or Light Shade	6.5-7.5
Raspberries	3	Full Sun or Light Shade	5.5-6.5
Rhubarb	4	Full Sun	6.0-6.8
Rosemary	6	Full Sun	6.0-7.0
Sage	4	Full Sun or Light Shade	6.0-7.0
Serviceberries	2-3	Full Sun or Light Shade	5.5-7.0
Strawberries	4-5	Full Sun	5.5-6.5
Thyme	5	Full Sun or Light Shade	5.5-7.0

*Grow cold tolerant varieties like Sweet Sixteen, Haralred and Honeycrisp

**Blueberries are very picky about their pH. Don't try to grow unless you have an acidic soil of 5.0 or lower.

Altitude

Your first and last frost date data (as mentioned above) is based on your zip code. If within your zip code, there are significant differences in altitude you may have to adjust those dates. While there are many factors affecting weather and altitude, in general the temperature goes down 3-6°F for every 1000 feet in altitude gain.

Since your spring and fall frost dates are estimates to begin with, it's fine to take a guess when you adjust them for your altitude. Be conservative at first, and then over the years refine your estimate as you have a better understanding of your unique climate.

Hills and Valleys

Sometimes it's not always as simple as the higher up you go, the colder it gets. While this is accurate on the macro scale, it is not necessarily true when comparing individual hills and valleys. In fact, some nights a valley may be as much as twenty degrees colder than the surrounding ridge.

The reason air temperature generally gets colder at high

Fig. 2 Napa cabbage. Know your first and last frost dates to avoid this!

elevations is because higher elevations have less pressurized air, and the less pressurized the air is, the colder it will be. And while the effect of pressure on air temperature is significant when comparing a thousand-foot difference in altitude, it doesn't play as much of a role when comparing the hundred-foot difference of a valley and a ridge.

Therefore, if the effect of air pressure is taken out of the equation, you are left with the fact that hot air rises and cold air sinks. This topic gets a bit more complicated as you take into account the physical landscape and the weather patterns on any given night, but in general, if you live in a valley, don't be surprised if your garden gets colder than your neighbor's garden on the hill.

Fig. 3
Cold Fog
Sinking Into
The Valley

Sun and Shade

The amount of direct sun your garden receives has a significant effect on how quickly your garden warms up in the morning and how hot it gets during the day. If part of your garden is in full or partial shade from a tree or building, it will take longer during the day, if ever, to reach the same temperature as the full sun areas right next to it.

As well, if your garden is on a slope or a hill it may

receive more or less sunlight at different times of the day. A garden on the north-facing side of a hill or ridge may only get a couple of hours of sunlight per day, while a garden on the south-facing side is likely to receive full sun the entire day. If your garden is on the eastern side of a hill, it likely receives intense morning sun, and early afternoon shade. Inversely, a western slope may be shaded in the morning, but have sun late into the afternoon.

Radiant Heat from Buildings

Another factor affecting your garden's climate is the radiant heat created if part or all of your garden is bordered by your home or another heated building. The radiant heat from that building can provide an extra five or more degrees of warmth. This extra heat will have an impressive effect on your garden climate.

If you plant near a building, make sure your plants receive enough sunlight and are not shaded by the building. This means you'll preferably want to plant on the south side of the building where it gets the most sun, or possibly the east or west sides, if growing shade-tolerant crops.

Your Soil

Just as important as the climate above ground is the soil below. Creating and maintaining healthy soil may feel like a daunting task. After all, there is a near unlimited amount of information to learn about soil, and many people devote their entire academic lives to it. With this much information it may feel unrealistic to do any more than sprinkle a little generic fertilizer every year and hope for the best. And while that technique will yield results, with just a little more effort you can have a profoundly more productive garden.

The two steps necessary to understand your soil are to identify its texture and to obtain a soil test from a lab. Once you do these two things, improving your soil is much easier. While it is always helpful to know more, you truly do not need to be a soil scientist or read their complicated books to manage healthy garden soil.

Soil Texture

The majority of soil is comprised of minerals broken down from rocks over thousands of years. The size of these minerals varies from large (sand), to medium (silt), to fine (clay). Most soils have all three particle sizes, but it's your garden's unique proportions of these particles that determine how your plants grow and how they respond to rain and irrigation.

Fig. 4
Soil with a High Clay Content

Clay, the smallest particle, has the least space in between the individual particles. Because clay particles are so tightly packed together, it can be difficult for roots to grow and for air and water to penetrate deep into the earth. However, once clay soil does absorb water, it is the slowest to dry out, which can be good for some plants and cause rot in others. Clay can be a challenging soil to garden with, but it is also the most prone to containing a high nutrient and organic matter content, which are key components of plant growth.

Sand, the largest particle, is the inverse of clay. Since there is so much space in between the individual particles, air, water, and roots can easily penetrate deep into the soil. The challenge with sandy soil is that it dries out very fast, and it is the least prone to having a high nutrient and organic matter content.

Silt, the medium-sized particle, is the middle ground

between clay and sand and tends to have characteristics of both.

With a little care, plants can grow and be happy with any proportion of these minerals, but an ideal soil composition is approximately 40% sand, 40% silt and 20% clay.

Soil Band Test: To get an idea of your soil texture, give it a feel. Take a small handful from your garden and get it wet but not dripping (fig.5a). Then spread out a bit of it between your thumb and index finger. If you can make a thin band of soil roughly an inch wide and two inches long without it breaking then your soil has a lot of clay in it (fig.5b). If that band won't form in the slightest then it has a high sand content (fig.5c). This is a very basic test to give you an idea of what you're working with.

This test along with some first-hand knowledge of growing in your specific soil may be all you need to understand to work with your soil type, but if you want a more precise measurement, you'll want to use the jar test, which is discussed below.

Fig. 5
Soil Band
Test
a. Wet Soil Ready for Testing
b. Clayey Soil Forming a Long Band
c. Sandy Soil Crumbling

a.   b.   c.

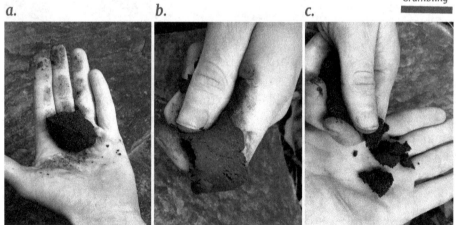

Jar Test: The jar test is an easy test to perform at home that determines the exact proportions of clay, silt and sand in your garden soil. To perform this test, you'll need a straight-walled transparent jar with a lid. A quart-sized mason jar is perfect. The first step is to obtain a soil sample by collecting soil from three or more different spots in your garden

Clay
8mm
10%

Silt
40mm
51%

Sand
30mm
39%

Fig. 6
Jar Test
a. Before
b. After

(collected at a depth of 2-6 inches). Mix the samples together to ensure you have an accurate representation of your garden. However, if you suspect there are significant variations in soil types throughout the garden, then do separate jar tests for each area.

Once you've collected the sample, fill the jar halfway with the soil, and then fill the jar until it is nearly full with water, leaving two inches of space at the top (fig.6a). Adding a teaspoon of Borax, dishwasher detergent, or regular soap will help the soil particles separate, however doing so is optional, and the experiment will work without it.

Put the lid on the jar, shake it for two minutes, and then leave it to rest somewhere undisturbed for 24 hours.

At this point, there should be three distinct sections of soil (fig.6b). The bottom section is sand, the middle is silt, and the top is clay. The water on top of the clay section may still be a bit murky. This is from small amounts of clay that have yet to settle and will not significantly affect the experiment. There may also be material floating around the top of the jar. This is organic matter and can be ignored for this experiment.

Using a ruler, measure the depth of each section of soil

and plug it into the equations below to get your sand, silt, and clay percentages.

Sand% = Depth of Sand Layer / Total Depth of Soil x 100
Silt% = Depth of Silt Layer / Total Depth of Soil x 100
Clay% = Depth of Clay Layer / Total Depth of Soil x 100

With these numbers you can now use fig. 7 to determine your precise soil type.

Most people do not have that ideal 40%-40%-20% soil type, but that does not mean you can't improve your soil and have an incredible garden. In chapter 7 (p. 66) you will learn how to manage and improve your soil.

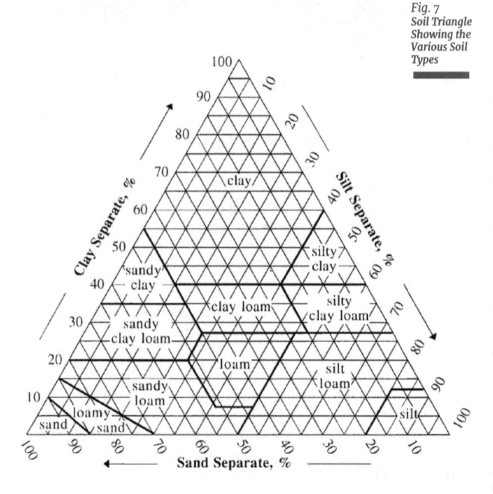

Fig. 7
Soil Triangle Showing the Various Soil Types

Nutrients, Organic Matter, and pH

While mineral particles make up the majority of your soil, it's the proportionally smaller quantities of specific nutrients and organic matter that provide the building blocks for a healthy plant. The best way to determine your soil's nutrient and organic matter content is to get your soil tested at a lab. Getting a soil test is very easy and affordable, normally costing around $20-$30.

If you have a local agriculture extension office, they frequently provide soil tests, and if there is no local testing facility near you, you can mail in your samples utilizing an online site. Most testing facilities offer multiple testing options, but unless you are really excited to learn about soil, their "basic" garden soil test will give you plenty of information.

When you get your soil test back, there will be a lot of information, as well as recommendations on how to improve any nutrient deficiencies. Thanks to these recommendations you can get by without understanding the intricacies of the test, however a little knowledge can also help you appreciate the complexity and beauty of your garden soil. Only continue reading in this section if you're curious. Otherwise rely on those soil report recommendations.

Macronutrients: Below are the three most important nutrients for your garden. Nine times out of ten if there's a nutrient deficiency in your soil, it is nitrogen, potassium or phosphorus.

- *Nitrogen*: This is the primary nutrient responsible for vegetative (leaf and stem) growth. It is one of the main components in chlorophyll, the compound used to convert sunlight into energy for the plants.
- *Phosphorus*: This is the primary nutrient responsible for root development and flower production.
- *Potassium*: This helps keep the cells within the plant strong and healthy. It also helps the plant withstand environmental stressors like extreme heat, cold, and drought.

Micronutrients: These are needed in much smaller quantities in your soil. They are also the least likely to cause you problems.

Unless your soil test specifically says your soil is deficient in a micronutrient you don't have to worry about these. The specific micronutrients that a soil lab will test for varies, but the most common are zinc, iron, copper, magnesium, and boron.

- *Zinc*: This helps in the production of chlorophyll.
- *Iron*: This helps in the production of chlorophyll.
- *Copper*: This helps with plant photosynthesis and metabolism. It is a component of many plant enzymes and therefore is important to plant growth and strength.
- *Magnesium*: This helps with many plant functions but most importantly the production of chlorophyll.
- *Boron*: This is necessary for seed development, cell division and the transportation of sugar throughout the plant.

Table 2
Ideal pH Ranges of Common Vegetables

Plant	pH	Continued		Continued	
Asparagus	6.0-8.0	Dill	5.5-6.5	Peas	6.0-7.5
Basil	5.5-7.0	Eggplant	5.5-7.0	Peppers	5.5-7.0
Beans	6.0-7.5	Garlic	5.5-7.5	Potatoes	5.0-6.5
Beets	6.5-8.0	Kale	6.0-7.5	Radish	6.0-7.5
Bok Choi	6.0-7.5	Kohlrabi	6.0-7.5	Rutabaga	6.0-7.5
Broccoli	6.0-7.5	Leeks	6.0-7.5	Spinach	6.0-7.5
Brussels Sprouts	6.0-7.5	Lettuce	6.0-7.5	Summer Squash	6.0-7.5
Cabbage	6.0-7.5	Melons	6.0-7.0	Sweet Potato	5.0-6.0
Cauliflower	6.0-7.5	Mustard Greens	6.0-7.5	Swiss Chard	6.0-7.0
Carrots	5.5-7.0	Napa Cabbage	6.0-7.5	Tomatoes	5.5-7.5
Cilantro	6.0-7.0	Onions	6.0-7.5	Turnips	6.0-7.5
Corn	5.5-7.5	Parsley	5.5-6.0	Winter Squash	6.0-7.5
Cucumbers	5.5-7.0	Parsnips	5.5-7.0	Zucchini	6.0-7.5

Organic Matter: This along with the three macronutrients, are the most important numbers to look at on your soil report. While organic matter is literally just decaying plant and/or animal material, it can have incredible effects in your garden. Organic matter improves soil structure, enhances water drainage, feeds beneficial microorganisms and insects, and provides nutrients to the plants at a healthy rate. A healthy garden soil has a range of 3-8% organic matter.

pH: This is a measure of the acidity and alkalinity of your soil. Every plant has a different ideal pH range (table 2). Outside of this range, certain nutrients become unavailable to the plant, and their health suffers.

Improving Your Soil

If your garden soil is less than ideal by any of these specific measures, there are always ways to amend your soil and make your plants happier. Refer to chapter 7 (p. 66) to learn how to improve your soil.

Your Garden Plan 2

In some low altitude areas, the growing conditions are so ideal for vegetables that having a garden is as simple as sprinkling a few seeds, weeding once or twice, and then reaping the rewards. The ease of these gardens may seem appealing, but there is also something deeply fulfilling about taking a cold, windy, dry climate and creating an oasis of food. To do this, however, you will need to form a solid plan.

A good garden plan doesn't need to feel like homework. Late winter, when the garden may still be covered in snow, is a wonderful time to take out a notebook and a seed catalog and start dreaming up a plan. This is an ideal time to get excited about the little world you will create as soon as the weather warms. Garden planning is a beautiful task where logic and creativity come together and will hopefully be cherished rather than thought of as a chore.

What to Grow

Possibly the most exciting question to ask yourself is what you want to grow. To help figure this out, I recommend looking through seed catalogs (either physical or online). In this section we'll explore some factors to consider when deciding what vegetables are right for your garden.

Days to Maturity

By the time you're looking through seed catalogs, you should know roughly how long your growing season is, as discussed in the "Your Climate" section (p. 7). With this information, you can immediately tell if you have enough growing days to accommodate a certain vegetable's growth. But also keep in mind that there can be significant differences between varieties of the same vegetable. For example, tomato

Easy	Medium	Hard
Asparagus	Beans	Eggplant
Beets	Broccoli	Melons
Cabbage	Brussels Sprouts	Peppers
Bok Choi	Cauliflower	Sweet Potato
Napa Cabbage	Corn	Tomatoes
Carrots	Cucumbers	Winter Squash
Kale	Leeks	
Kohlrabi	Onions	
Lettuce	Parsnips	
Peas	Potatoes	
Radish	S. Squash/Zucchini	
Rutabaga	Basil	
Turnips	Garlic	
Spinach		
Swiss Chard		
Mustard/ Asian Greens		
Cilantro		
Dill		
Perennial Herbs		
Parsley		

Table 1
Ease and Difficulty of Growing Common Vegetables at High Altitudes

plants vary from 50-90 days to maturity. Therefore, if you only have 80 days of frost-free weather, make sure to pick the right variety.

As well, many vegetables can be planted long before the last spring frost and continue growing well after the first fall frost. For example, Brussels sprouts may take 110 days to mature, but they are cold tolerant, so you can plant them a month before the last spring frost and they will continue to grow a month after the first fall frost.

Seed catalogs generally tell you how long before the last spring frost you can plant a certain variety. Below is also a list of common vegetables and whether they are frost tolerant or not.

Fig. 1 Even after a light frost cabbage will continue growing

Succession Planting

Succession planting is when you plant and grow a certain crop at multiple times throughout the season. Instead of one short harvest period, by planting multiple successions you can have a long, continuous harvest, or a series of multiple shorter harvests. This may mean planting lettuces every week, or having two separate broccoli plantings, two weeks apart.

No Frost Tolerance	Light Frost Tolerance	Moderate Frost Tolerance	Perennial or Able to Overwinter
Basil	Beets	Brussels Sprouts	Asparagus
Beans	Bok Choi	Cabbage	Garlic
Corn	Broccoli	Carrots	Parsley
Cucumbers	Cilantro	Cauliflower	Parsnips
Eggplant	Dill	Kale	Perennial Herbs
Melons	Lettuce	Kohlrabi	
Peppers	Mustard/ Asian Greens	Leeks	
Potatoes	Napa Cabbage	Onions	
S. Squash/Zucchini	Spinach	Peas	
Sweet Potato	Swiss Chard	Radish	
Tomatoes		Rutabaga	
Winter Squash		Turnips	

Table 2 Frost Tolerance of Common Vegetables

At high altitudes, the growing season is frequently so short that the challenge can be simply to get one succession to grow rather than multiple. However, with cold weather crops, there still may be time in the season to have multiple successions. Refer to the Plant Index (p. 138) or the "Days to Maturity" on your seed packet to determine if there is time to grow more than one successions.

Sun Requirements

Most vegetables are happiest with full sun, but that is not always possible. Seed catalogs will tell you whether a variety can grow in light shade, partial shade, or full shade. A good rule of thumb is that if you harvest the leaves from a plant, like kale, lettuce, and herbs, they will be at least moderately tolerant of growing in partial or light shade. The next most tolerant are root crops. The least shade tolerant are fruiting vegetables such as tomatoes, cucumbers, and peppers.

Keep in mind that even if a plant grows well in shade, it will likely take longer to mature than what is stated in the catalog. The catalog's "Days to Maturity" number assumes ideal conditions, so anything less than ideal will add extra days to that estimate. Therefore, if you need to grow vegetables in partial or light shade, make sure to give some buffer time at the end of the season.

Gardeners and botanists sometimes have conflicting terminology. For a botanist, an annual is a plant that goes from a seed to producing new seeds within one year, and after producing those seeds, its life cycle naturally ends. A biennial is a plant that takes two years to produce seeds before dying. And a perennial is a plant that can survive for multiple years and goes through more than one seed-producing cycle in its life.

Gardeners, unlike botanists, typically refer to plants as annuals if they are only grown for one season in their garden, even if they potentially could survive for longer. For example, in their native tropical climate, peppers are perennials and live for multiple years, but since they die from a frost they are frequently grown in northern gardens as if they were annuals. As well, carrots are biennials that produce a seed in their second year of life, but gardeners normally harvest their carrots in the fall before the plant has a chance to produce a seed the following year. To a gardener, peppers and carrots are annuals despite technically being perennials and biennials.

Throughout this book if I refer to a plant as an annual, I am doing so as a gardener and mean that it is planted, harvested, and dies all in the same season.

Hybrid and Heirloom Varieties

There are some misconceptions out there around what hybrid seeds are. People associate hybrid varieties with GMOs (genetically modified organisms) or other unnatural processes. This is inaccurate. Hybrids are merely a more intricate and modern take on the plant selection methods used for thousands of years.

      This traditional plant selection method, which is used to make heirloom varieties, consists of choosing the healthiest, tastiest and most productive plants to save seeds from. This human influenced version of natural selection gradually leads to a plant that is ideally suited for the environment it is being grown in. Hybrids, however are created by breeding two characteristically different varieties of a plant to make a "hybrid" variety that has the best parts of its two parents. This is a very simplified explanation of hybrids, but the most important takeaway is that there is no genetic modification involved, or anything more "unnatural" than the process for creating heirlooms. Sometimes an heirloom variety is the best choice to grow, and other times a hybrid is.

Fig. 2 Grow Heirloom Varieties if You plan to Save Seeds

      Hybrids have a lot going for them and are frequently more productive plants, but there are two factors that can make an heirloom a better choice in your garden. The first is when an heirloom has been specifically bred for high altitudes or cold climates. For hundreds of years, before the advent of seed companies, family farms saved their own seeds to create heirloom varieties that were uniquely suited for their climate. Nowadays, seed companies breed hybrids for their largest customer groups, which are generally not high altitude gardeners. Therefore, if you find an heirloom variety that is specifically bred for your climate, it very well may grow better for you than any hybrid variety will.

The second factor that makes heirlooms a better choice than hybrids is their taste. Frequently, when developing hybrid varieties, farmers and scientists choose productivity over taste. This can result in a highly productive plant that doesn't have a lot of flavor. Generally, hybrid varieties still taste good, but maybe not quite as great as heirloom varieties.

Sidebar 2
The Myth of GMO Vegetables

The final note to be aware of with hybrids is that if you save seeds from a hybrid plant, those seeds will revert back to their parent's characteristics, or something altogether different. Therefore, if you plan on saving your own seeds you should start with an heirloom variety.

Variety Gimmicks

These days there are enormous amounts of seed variety options. There are purple cauliflower, white carrots, and exotically shaped squash. All of these strange and interesting varieties can be a lot of fun to grow, but they are also likely to be less productive, and less tasty than their more traditional counterparts.

When a farmer saves seed, they choose the

There is a false belief out there that all vegetables could be grown as GMOs (genetically modified organisms). In reality, there are relatively few types of GMOs and even fewer that are available to be grown in a vegetable garden. The ten genetically modified plants available in the US market are: summer squash, cotton, soybean, corn, papaya, alfalfa, sugar beets, canola, potatoes, and apples. Of those ten, only squash, corn, and potatoes are likely to be grown in a home vegetable garden. And even with squash, corn, and potatoes, it is unlikely that you could actually find the GMO versions of these crops for sale on a retail seed website or at a nursery. Genetically modified varieties tend to be isolated at the moment to large industrial farms.

GMOs are becoming more available in the US regularly. Someday we may need to be more careful of the seeds we buy for our garden, but at the moment our garden plot will easily remain GMO free.

individual plants to save seeds from based on certain criteria. Normally, the main criteria for saving seeds is taste and productivity, with the secondary, less important criteria being pest resistance and appearance. However, when you make appearance the most important criteria you do so at the expense of taste and productivity. If a purple cauliflower excites you, then grow it. Just know that it may take longer to grow, produce a smaller head, and not taste quite as good.

Where in the Garden to Plant

Most gardens are not perfectly uniform. There are areas within the garden that have uniquely different growing conditions. When creating your garden plan, ask yourself, does every area of the garden get the same amount of sun? Is the soil the same throughout the whole garden? And are there any physical objects in the garden, such as walls, fences, or large

Sidebar 3
Note Taking

Unless you have an incredible memory, taking good notes is essential for a productive and healthy garden. Note taking should start before the season begins, as you form a comprehensive garden plan. These notes will include when, what, and where to plant, as well as how much and what kind of fertilizer to apply.

As the season progresses, note taking becomes even more important. The notes you take throughout the season will help you remember what worked and what didn't, so that in following years your garden will be even more productive. These types of notes may be about adjusting planting dates or plant spacing, how a certain pest or disease treatment worked, or how you were disappointed with a certain variety and will want to try a new one.

My recommendation is to have a dedicated garden journal where you take notes about everything that happens in your garden. One of the most beautiful aspects of gardening is the adjustments and fine tuning you do from year to year. I know from personal experience there are few things as frustrating as thinking I'll remember a piece of information about the garden, only to forget it by the time I start planning for the next year's garden.

rocks? Depending on your answers, some areas may be better suited for certain crops than other areas. If you have an area of partial shade, make sure to plant shade-tolerant crops. If you have one area of the garden that has more clay than another, plant clay-tolerant crops. If you have a fence or a wall in the garden, you may want to set up a trellis and grow plants that like to climb.

Tall and Short Plants

Another factor to consider is the effect the individual plants have on each other. If you grow tall plants like tomatoes or peppers be aware that, depending on where they are in the garden, they may shade out shorter plants behind them. For this reason, it's helpful to grow your tallest plants on the north side of the garden, so they are not in between the sun and the rest of your garden.

Fig. 3 Lettuce, Carrots and Onions are Good Companion Plants

Companion Planting

One of the more interesting yet controversial topics in gardening is companion planting. This is the idea that certain plants grow better or worse depending on the other types of plants in close proximity to them. While companion planting is a fascinating topic, in regard to garden vegetables, its efficacy is mostly based on folk accounts and not backed by reliable science. However, just because something is yet to be quantified and understood by science, that does not mean we

need to disregard hundreds of years of experience-based accounts. It is really up to you if you want to incorporate companion planting into your garden plan. It may help, it may not, but it probably won't hurt.

Refer to Table 3 for a list of the companion plants for common garden vegetables.

	Companions	Incompatible
Asparagus	Basil, Beets, Lettuce, Parsley, Spinach, Tomato	
Basil	Peppers, Tomatoes	Cucumbers, Beans
Beans	Broccoli, Cabbage, Carrots, Cauliflower, Celery, Corn, Cucumbers, Eggplant, Peas, Potatoes, Radishes, Squash, Strawberries, Tomatoes	Garlic, Onions, Peppers, Sunflowers
Beets	Asparagus, Broccoli, Cauliflower, Lettuce, Onion	Mustard Greens, Pole Beans
Broccoli	Beans, Beets, Celery, Cucumbers, Onions, Potatoes, Sage	Cabbage, Cauliflower, Lettuce, Pole Bean, Tomatoes
Brussels Sprouts	Dill, Lettuce, Radishes, Sage, Spinach, Turnips	Tomatoes
Cabbage	Beans, Celery, Cucumbers, Dill, Kale, Lettuce, Onions, Potatoes, Sage, Spinach, Thyme	Broccoli, Cauliflower, Strawberries, Tomatoes
Carrots	Beans, Lettuce, Onions, Peas, Radishes, Rosemary, Sage, Tomatoes	Dill, Parsley
Cauliflower	Beans, Beets, Celery, Cucumbers, Sage, Thyme	Broccoli, Cabbage, Strawberry, Tomato

Table 3 Companion Planting

Table 3
Companion
Planting
Continued

	Companions	Incompatible
Cilantro	Eggplant, Potato, Tomato	
Corn	Beans, Cucumbers, Lettuce, Melons, Peas, Potato, Squash, Sunflower	Tomatoes
Cucumbers	Beans, Broccoli, Cabbage, Cauliflower, Corn, Lettuce, Peas, Radishes, Sunflowers	Perennial Herbs, Melons, Potatoes
Dill	Broccoli, Brussels Sprouts, Cabbage, Cauliflower, Kale	Carrots, Tomatoes
Eggplant	Basil, Beans, Lettuce, Peas, Potatoes, Spinach	
Garlic	Beets, Broccoli, Brussels Sprouts, Cabbage, Cauliflower, Kale, Celery, Lettuce, Tomatoes	Beans, Peas
Kale	Cabbage, Dill, Potatoes, Rosemary, Sage	Strawberries, Tomatoes
Kohlrabi	Cabbage, Dill, Potatoes, Rosemary, Sage	Strawberries, Tomatoes
Leeks	Onions, Celery, Carrots	
Lettuce	Asparagus, Beets, Brussels Sprouts, Cabbage, Carrots, Corn, Cucumbers, Eggplant, Onions, Peas, Potatoes, Radishes, Spinach, Strawberries, Sunflowers, Tomatoes	Broccoli
Melons	Corn, Nasturtiums, Peas, Radishes, Sunflowers, Tomatoes	Cucumbers, Potatoes
Onions	Beets, Broccoli, Cabbage, Carrots, Lettuce, Peppers, Potatoes, Spinach, Tomatoes	Beans, Peas, Sage

Table 3
Companion
Planting
Continued

	Companions	Incompatible
Parsley	Asparagus, Corn, Peppers, Tomatoes	
Parsnips	Peas, Potatoes, Beans, Radish, Garlic	Carrots, Celery
Peas	Beans, Carrots, Corn, Cucumbers, Eggplant, Lettuce, Melons, Parsnips, Potatoes, Radishes, Spinach, Turnips	Garlic, Onions
Peppers	Basil, Cilantro, Onions, Spinach, Tomatoes	Beans
Potatoes	Beans, Broccoli, Cabbage, Corn, Eggplant, Garlic, Kale, Lettuce, Onions, Peas, Radishes	Cucumbers, Melons, Squash, Sunflowers, Tomatoes, Turnips
Spinach	Asparagus, Brussels Sprouts, Cabbage, Celery, Dill, Eggplant, Lettuce, Onions, Peas, Peppers, Radishes, Strawberries, Tomatoes	
Summer Squash/ Zucchini	Celery, Corn, Melon	Potatoes
Swiss Chard	Cabbage, Carrots, Lettuce, Onions, Beets	Beans
Tomatoes	Asparagus, Basil, Beans, Carrots, Celery, Dill, Lettuce, Melons, Onions, Parsley, Peppers, Radishes, Spinach, Thyme	Broccoli, Brussels Sprouts, Cabbage, Cauliflower, Corn, Kale, Potatoes
Winter Squash	Celery, Corn, Melon	Potatoes

Crop Rotation

Crop rotation is when you don't grow the same crop in the same place for multiple years in a row. The first reason for rotating your crops is that different crop families (see table 4) take different amounts of nutrients from the soil, and by moving them throughout the garden, your soil won't become overly deficient in one area. The other reason for crop rotation is that different plants attract different pests and diseases. By moving your plants, pests and diseases have a more difficult time finding their desired host. While crop rotation can be very helpful in certain situations, it has frequently been overly praised as a necessity for a healthy garden. The benefits of crop rotation are real, but those benefits can frequently be accomplished by easier means.

In regard to nutrient deficiency, a soil test tells you how much fertilizer and compost your garden needs. If you stay on top of your garden's soil health, you can grow the same crop in the same spot year after year without negative effects on the soil. After all, perennial plants stay in the same place for years with great results.

Crop rotation is a great tool for dealing with insects and disease from year to year, however if your garden is small and isolated from other gardens, it's likely you could go years without encountering a serious insect or disease issue. Instead of preemptively rotating crops, it is easier to keep a close eye on your plants and, if a problem arises, address it then. Preventative crop rotation is only mildly helpful, therefore only do it if you're motivated.

There are times when crop rotation can actually do more harm than good. For example, there may be a spot in the garden that is uniquely suited for a certain crop (like growing kale in a partially shaded corner, or peas near a trellis). If you feel obligated to regularly rotate your plants, you may not be able to grow your plants in their ideal location.

Crop rotation is a great tool to know and utilize, but it is not your only option.

Preparing Your Garden Beds

When planning your garden, it is important to decide how to prepare the soil for planting. Soil that is ready for planting is weed-free and well aerated. The two ways you accomplish this are through either *till* or *no-till* methods.

Till

When you till your soil, you mix and disturb the top section of soil (anywhere from three inches to two feet). On farms, this is generally done with a tractor, but at home it is most frequently accomplished with a shovel, hoe, or walk behind rototiller.

Table 4
Plant Families

Crop Family	Plants
Solanaceae (Nightshade Family)	Eggplants, Peppers, Potatoes, Tomatoes
Brassicaceae (Brassica Family)	Bok Choi, Broccoli, Brussels Sprouts, Cabbage, Cauliflower, Kale, Kohlrabi, Mustard/Asian Greens, Napa Cabbage, Radish, Rutabaga, Turnips
Cucurbitaceae (Cucurbit Family)	Cucumbers, Melons, Summer Squash/Zucchini, Winter Squash
Fabaceae (Legume Family)	Beans, Peas
Amaryllidaceae (Allium Family)	Garlic, Leeks, Onions
Chenopodiaceae (Goosefoot Family)	Beets, Spinach, Swiss Chard
Umbelliferae (Umbel Family)	Carrots, Cilantro, Dill, Parsley, Parsnips
Other	Basil (Mint Family), Corn (Gramineae/Grass Family), Lettuce (Aster Family), Sweet Potatoes (Convolvulaceae/ Morning Glory Family), Asparagus (Asparagaceae Family)

The benefits of tilling your soil are that it buries and kills most of your weeds, as well as aerating or "fluffing up" the soil which improves water and air flow, and allows plant roots to grow through the soil easier. This technique also allows soil amendments like compost and fertilizer to be easily integrated into the soil at the time of tillage.

The drawbacks of tilling your soil are associated with the degradation of your garden's natural soil structure. It may seem like soil is one finely packed substance, but in reality, undisturbed soil has many unique pathways for air, water, and roots to travel through. By tilling the soil, you are essentially mashing up the soil and destroying these pathways. Once destroyed it can take years for them to form again. This means that once you "fluff up" the soil, after a year of natural compaction from rain and other elements, the soil becomes more compacted than before you initially tilled. In the end, you may find yourself in a cycle where you must re-till the soil every year to keep it aerated.

While tilling has its drawbacks, it is also the most commonly used method for preparing a garden bed because it works. It is especially helpful when you start a new garden and must get rid of grass or other weeds that are well established and have been there for years.

Fig. 4 Turning the Soil with a Shovel

No-Till

No-till gardening utilizes the already existing air, water, and root pathways within your soil. When done right, no-till bed prep is easier than tilling, because it does not require you to dig up your soil every year. However, with no-till gardening you need to be more attentive to weeding since you can't simply bury them underground every year like you do with tilled beds.

Managing weeds can be especially difficult when preparing a new no-till area for gardening. You can always prep the new area by hand-pulling the weeds, however this can be an intensive and time-consuming task.

Another option is called *sheet mulching* which is when you lay cardboard over the garden area and then cover the cardboard with at least a 3 inches of soil. Within a few months to a year, the cardboard and the weeds underneath will have decomposed and you will have a weed free no-till bed ready for planting.

Another option is if you are planning on using framed

Fig. 5
Sheet
Mulching

garden beds that are at least eight inches high, you can build the frame directly on top of the weeds and then fill in the frame with new soil. Except for the most vigorous weeds, everything underneath the soil will be smothered and die.

Another concern is how to incorporate compost and fertilizer into no-till beds. Luckily in most situations it is fine to leave the fertilizer and compost on the surface and let it slowly work into the earth through the efforts of insects and rain.

Sidebar 4
Is it a Fruit or a Vegetable?

We've all heard that line about how a tomato is a fruit and not a vegetable. And while it is a fun statement, it's not actually true. In reality, a tomato is a fruit *and* a vegetable. Fruits and vegetables are not mutually exclusive terms.

Fruit is a scientific term to describe the fleshy part of a plant that contains a seed. By this definition a fruit would include a watermelon, orange, and apple, as well as a tomato, pepper, and cucumber. Vegetable on the other hand is not a scientific term, but instead a cultural one. Therefore, the definition of a vegetable is a little looser. A vegetable is a part of a plant used for food, generally in salty or savory dishes. By this definition kale, potatoes, and carrots are all vegetables, as well as tomatoes, peppers, and cucumbers. When comparing a scientific fruit to a cultural vegetable there is overlap.

Things get complicated when the word fruit veers away from its scientific definition and starts to have its own cultural definition. Culturally, a fruit is an edible, sweet part of a plant that can be eaten alone or used to make a dessert. By this definition a tomato would probably not be a fruit.

So, the next time someone tells you a tomato is a fruit and not a vegetable, feel free to correct them.

Part Two

Challenges and Their Solutions

Cold Weather and a Short Growing Season 3

Possibly the biggest challenge facing high altitude gardeners is cold and erratic temperatures. Where low-landers might enjoy six months or more of frost-free weather, a high altitude gardener on a similar latitude might have three months or less. And even during those three months, summer nights will likely get significantly colder than their sea level counterparts. But just because you might get snow in May and hail in August doesn't mean you can't have a productive and fun garden that outperforms gardens in more mild climates.

With the advice and techniques in this chapter, you can reap the rewards of a cold weather climate and mitigate the challenges.

Crop Choice

On page 20 I discuss the importance of choosing the right types of vegetables and the right varieties of those vegetables. This is an extremely important step when working with a short, cold growing season. Some plants love cool summer nights while others merely tolerate them. Some plants grow better after a light frost while others won't survive. Some varieties of the same plant may take 100 days to mature while others may take 70. Take your time and choose carefully. The choices you make before planting your first seeds are the most important. You can do everything right, and employ every trick in this book, but if you're growing a plant that's incompatible with your climate it won't produce well.

In the end, the vegetables and varieties you choose are specific to your garden and your preferences. Even though kale is an excellent cold weather plant, if you don't like it, you probably won't want to grow it. And if tomatoes are your favorite vegetable, even though they are a bit more challenging to grow, it'll be worth it for you to try.

Fig. 1
Cucumber
Transplants

Transplant vs. Direct Seed

Transplanting is when you take a plant that was seeded into a small container, in a greenhouse or on a windowsill, and plant it in your garden as an already formed plant. Direct seeding is planting the vegetable seeds directly into your garden. Both techniques have their pros and cons, but if you have a short growing season, using transplants, when possible, is an excellent way to give your plants 3 to 8 weeks of extra growing time when the outside temperatures are otherwise too cold.

If you're lucky enough to have a greenhouse, or a very sunny southern exposure windowsill, you can grow your own transplants, but if not, you can purchase many varieties of transplants from your local nursery.

Some crops have sensitive root systems and need direct seeding rather than being transplanted. Refer to the Plant Index (p. 138) to learn which vegetables can and can't be transplanted.

Planting Near Your Home

If you grow plants next to your home, the radiant heat from the building creates a uniquely warm microclimate. Depending on how much sun your plants need, you will have the most success growing on the sunny, southern side of the building, however some shade-tolerant crops may do well in other locations.

Even if you can't have proper garden beds against your house, you may still be able to have a few potted plants growing next to the building.

Fig. 2
Weed Mat

Keep in mind that to get the most benefit from the radiant heat you need to have your plants very close to the building. Once you get five or ten feet away, the heating effects drastically reduce.

Weed Mat

Weed mat is a tarp-like fabric placed on the surface of a garden bed (fig. 2). Within it, there are strategically spaced holes allowing plants to be seeded or transplanted through it and into the soil. Weed mat is used to stop weeds, to keep the soil from drying out, and to warm up the soil earlier in the spring. The warming effect of a weed mat comes from the heat its black surface absorbs from the sun. This heat warms the soil directly below it, as well as the air directly above it, which is very beneficial for young plants in the spring.

The setup involved with weed mat is fairly intensive, but once in place, a good quality woven weed mat can last ten years.

Another option similar to weed mat is using black plastic to cover your beds. Unlike weed mat, which is made with woven fabric and is permeable to water, black plastic is not, and therefore drip tape (p. 52) needs to be placed underneath the plastic to water your plants.

As well, weeds more easily puncture and grow through black plastic. Because it is so easily punctured and ripped, it is generally used for only one season before being replaced, which creates a lot of waste.

Fig. 3
Row Cover

See page 263 for instructions on setting up your weed mat.

Row Cover

Row cover is a simple and effective tool that is well utilized by organic farmers, but largely underused by gardeners. It is a thin white fabric that is designed to be draped over your plants to keep them warm, retain moisture, keep away pests and diseases, and reduce the shock on transplanted veggies from the high altitude sun. It is thin enough to let sunlight and water through, yet still thick enough to prevent damage from freezing temperatures.

One of the more unique aspects of high altitude weather are the erratic late spring and early fall frosts. These frosts have the potential to kill many of your plants despite the weeks of frost-free weather you might experience before and after. While row cover won't keep your plants growing all through the winter, it can provide that extra bit of life-saving warmth when they need it most. Depending on the thickness of your row cover, it keeps the air around your plants up to eight degrees warmer.

As well, in many high altitude climates, even when there is no risk of a frost, the nighttime temperatures may never get above the 40s and 50s. And while some crops thrive in those cool summer nights, others simply tolerate them. A cucumber plant, for example, won't die from a 45-degree night, but it sure won't be happy. Row cover provides general warmth and creates a more hospitable microclimate for heat-loving plants throughout the growing season. For warm season crops, keeping them a few degrees warmer might not be essential, but it speeds up their growth and allows for a longer and more abundant harvest.

See page 258 for instructions on setting up your row cover.

Sidebar 1
Prioritizing Your Row Cover

I frequently find myself with a row cover shortage. I never seem to buy enough for all the plants that want it. Because of this, I end up prioritizing what plants need it the most. For example, I tend to cover my carrots throughout the season because it helps keep the ground squirrels from finding and eating them. But in the middle of September when there is the usual light frost warning, I take the row cover off the carrots (because they can handle a light frost) and put it over the winter squash that needs a couple more weeks of growth but will die from a frost. Once the risk of frost has passed, I put the row cover back on the carrots, and hope that a day without row cover wasn't long enough for the squirrels to find their favorite snack. If I had enough row cover, I'd keep both the carrots and the squash covered, but for me this works fine.

Raised Beds

A raised bed is a garden bed where the bed's soil is higher than the surrounding ground. The bed can be a couple of inches high, or a couple of feet. It can be contained in a frame or be a loose mound of soil. And while there are many ways to make a raised bed, the effect is similar: the above-ground soil warms up faster in the spring. This happens for the same reason a small ice cube melts faster than a larger block of ice. The smaller the object and the more surface area exposed to warmer air temperatures, the faster an object finds equilibrium with the air.

While a raised bed alone may only add a few degrees of soil warmth in the spring, that may translate into being able to plant a week earlier, which is a big deal when growing in a short season climate.

Something to keep in mind is that a raised bed will not affect the air temperature. A tomato plant will die in freezing weather regardless of how elevated the garden bed is, so choose cold-hardy plants when growing early in the season.

Fig. 4 Raised Beds Before Being Filled With Soil

Along with allowing you to get an earlier spring planting, a raised bed also helps with water drainage, weed prevention, back pain, and general aesthetics. While a raised bed alone may only provide a brief season extension, when coupled with all the other benefits, it might be right for your garden.

See page 261 for instructions on creating your raised beds.

Fig. 5 Raised Bed in the Snow

Fig. 6 A Raised Bed can be as High as you Desire

Cloches

Cloches are small, transparent glass or plastic coverings that are placed over a single plant and act as a mini greenhouse. They are a great way to protect individual cold intolerant plants when planting early in the spring. Cloches can be a great tool, but due to their small size the air within the cloche is prone to overheating if not well ventilated.

You can buy premade cloches or make your own using an old transparent milk or water jug. Simply cut off the bottom of the jug and place it over the plant. Remove the lid to allow ventilation, and put it back on when nights are expected to get especially cold (fig. 7).

Low Tunnels

Low tunnels are somewhere in between a greenhouse and row cover, and are an excellent way to extend your growing season into the early spring and late fall. They are made by using 4-feet high, 3-6 feet wide PVC or metal conduit hoops that are placed over the garden bed and spaced 5 feet apart. The hoops are then covered with one or two layers of greenhouse grade plastic.

Fig. 7-8 Cloches Made From Old Water Jugs

The plastic retains a significant amount of solar heat and can extend the growing season a month or more in the spring and fall. Since this method does not use an external heating source other than the sun, the temperatures may still drop below freezing. Therefore, you will have the best luck growing cold weather crops like kale, salad greens, or carrots.

One challenge with low tunnels is watering the plants. The plastic can be difficult to remove in order to access the plants, especially early or late in the season when it may be frozen to the ground. As well, in the early spring and late fall you may not have water access in your garden because of frozen hoses. Luckily, the plastic traps a lot of moisture, so you won't need to water frequently.

Another challenge is keeping the plants from overheating. If you don't provide ventilation and you leave the plastic covering over the bed too late in the spring or cover the bed too early in the fall, the temperatures can reach well over 100 degrees and can potentially kill the plants.

Sidebar 2
Excessive
Heat and
Premature
Bolting

While high altitude climates have a predominance of cool weather, that does not mean some high altitude areas can't experience intense summer heat. While many plants thrive in this heat, growing cool season crops in the middle of summer can cause a plant to bolt, which is when it prematurely goes from its vegetative phase to its flowering phase.

Once a plant enters its flowering phase, it stops putting its energy into root and leaf production, and as a result the flavor of the leaves and roots become less desirable. If you're harvesting the leaves or roots of a plant, you need that plant to stay in its vegetative phase for as long as possible.

Premature bolting can happen with many plants but occurs most frequently with short-season cold-weather annuals like arugula, radishes, mustard greens, and lettuce as well as some annual herbs like basil, cilantro, and dill. To stop the plant from bolting and to give it a longer vegetative phase, use row cover. Row cover blocks a small but significant portion of the sunlight which keeps the plant cool and in a vegetative phase for longer. Another alternative is to plant heat sensitive crops in partial shade to keep them cool.

Eventually, not even row cover or planting in the shade will stop the natural life cycle of the plant, and it will begin to flower. For some plants like basil you can pinch off any forming flowers, so the plant continues to put its energy toward the leaves, but for most plants once it begins to flower there is nothing more you can do besides harvest whatever is left and then replant.

Cold Frames

Cold frames are another option to extend your growing season. They provide a similar function to low tunnels but are generally smaller and are more permanent installations in the garden. Whereas low tunnels are covered in a thin flexible plastic, most cold frames are wood framed and covered with a hard polycarbonate plastic. Cold frame designs vary greatly, but most are slanted to face the sun and open with a hinged lid.

Like low tunnels, there is no added heat source beyond the sun. For this reason, if you experience intense winters, a cold frame will not be able to keep plants growing through the entire winter. Also, like low tunnels, there is a risk of the plants overheating on warm days. This problem is easily remedied by leaving the lid propped open or completely removing the lid for the summer months.

Fig. 9 Cold Frame

Greenhouses

While this book focuses mainly on the more traditional outdoor garden, the most effective solution to a cold climate is to have a greenhouse. With a greenhouse you are essentially creating a completely new climate that is only lightly tied to the outdoor weather.

With a greenhouse, whether heated or unheated, you can grow an amazing array of crops, many times throughout the entire winter. And while the benefits of a greenhouse are immense, constructing one can be a timely and expensive project. If you have the space, interest and funds, a greenhouse is an incredible addition to a garden, but not essential. An outdoor garden, even at high altitudes, can be profoundly productive.

Healthy Plants Grow Faster

If you have a short growing season, one solution is to have the plants simply grow faster, and the best way to do that is to keep them happy. A happy plant is a fast-growing plant. That means a well thought out garden plan (p. 20), consistent irrigation (p. 49), and healthy soil (p. 66).

Sidebar 3
Hail

Hail can be a wildcard in any season. In some high altitude climates hail is very rare, while in others there may be a hail storm every couple of weeks. The tough part about hail is that it can be unpredictable and there's no foolproof way to protect the plants from its destructive effects. Row cover can help against small hail, but if the hail is large enough it will rip through the fabric. If you know a storm is coming you can cover some plants with a bed sheet, which will provide more protection.

Dry and Arid Weather 4

When a plant gets the right amount of water it grows faster, produces more, and has a greater capacity to fight off attacks from pests and diseases. Water may seem like the simplest of amendments to your garden, but it is also one of the most important.

While high altitudes can get intense fog as well as rain storms that rival the tropics, most high altitude areas have a predominance of dry, arid weather. This low humidity and lack of rain can be especially challenging for gardeners when trying to keep their plants happy. However, with a few tricks, and an appropriate irrigation plan, low humidity and a lack of rain won't affect the productivity and health of your garden.

When to Water

In many lowland temperate areas there is enough rainfall that gardeners may be able to go the whole season without irrigating their garden. In dry climates, however, there is no escaping the need for irrigation. A good saturating rain storm should not be expected, but rather treated as a pleasant surprise. And even after that heavy rain does come, the soil will dry out quickly due to the low humidity. It's essential for a high altitude gardener to know when to water.

General Watering Rule

While the water needs of every type of plant are different, there is generally an overlapping sweet spot that most garden plants enjoy. If you'd like, you certainly can tailor your watering schedule to each specific type of plant, however this can be time-consuming and is not necessary for a productive and healthy garden.

Fig. 1 Water- logged Soil

A good rule of thumb for almost all plants is to water the garden when the soil is dry 1.5 inches deep into the ground. The easiest way to test this is to simply stick a finger into the soil and feel for moisture. In dry climates with well-drained soil and full sun, this translates to watering roughly three times per week (this is a very rough estimate that should be tailored to your specific garden).

Exceptions to the General Watering Rule

There are two main exceptions to this uniform watering technique. First, when you direct seed or transplant a vegetable they will need more frequent waterings until they develop roots that can reach deep into the soil to find water. This means keeping the soil around ungerminated seeds thoroughly watered until germination occurs, as well as watering newly germinated plants and transplants whenever the soil is dry down to the first 0.5 inches of soil, rather than 1.5 inches. Over the course of a week or two you can transition those newly germinated plants and transplants onto the same watering schedule as the rest of the garden.

The other time you may need to alter your watering schedule is if there are two very different types of soil in your garden. If half of your garden is sandy and the other half has a lot of clay, the sandy half will drain much faster. Having two drastically different soil types in a small area is unusual, but in this situation if you were to water everything on the same schedule, the clay section would remain waterlogged while the other half would dry out. Refer to page 12 to learn about your soil composition.

Sidebar 1

Regularly Reassess Your Watering Schedule

Keep Your Plants Growing Fast

While garden vegetables will likely survive the season on a once a week watering schedule, it will significantly slow their growth, and at high altitudes your growing season is likely to be too short to allow for a slow growing plant. Watering is not merely a way to keep a plant alive, but also one of the most important ways to allow them to flourish.

It's important to regularly reassess your watering schedule. As the seasons change and the plants grow, your garden may have different watering needs than it did earlier in the season. Keeping the soil moist 1.5 inches below the surface may require four waterings per week in July, and only two waterings per week in September.

How to Water

There is no wrong method for watering your garden. All methods have the potential to be just as effective. The most important factor is to enjoy whatever method of irrigation that you implement. This is not just because enjoying yourself is the whole point of having a garden, but also because if you don't like the task of irrigating your garden you will be less likely to actually do it, and the plants will suffer. With a well thought out plan, typically utilizing a sprinkler or drip irrigation, watering doesn't have to be a burden.

Watering with a Sprinkler

Using a sprinkler is a very easy method, which requires very little setup. And if you use a spigot timer, you can set the sprinkler to turn on and off without even being there. Sprinklers are very effective at providing a uniform amount of water, and distributing that water slowly enough that clay soils, weed mat, and row cover have time to absorb it.

*Fig. 2
Overhead
Sprinkler*

The downside of sprinklers is that they waste water through evaporation, and they may end up watering areas where nothing is growing. Running the sprinklers in the early morning gives the water plenty of time to be absorbed into the soil before the intense midday sun causes excessive evaporation.

Drip Irrigation

Drip irrigation is when you set up lines of flexible perforated plastic tubing alongside your plants (fig. 3). Drip irrigation can be an intricate and relatively complicated watering system to set up, but once done, it is the most effective and easiest to use.

Drip irrigation uses the least water of all the options because it directs water to the plant's root systems where water is needed the most. Because it delivers the water directly to the soil's surface, it is the ideal irrigation technique when using weed mat or row cover.

Also, when you use overhead watering, such as sprinklers or hand watering, you get the leaves of the plant wet, which can potentially spread disease. This is not a huge concern in dry climates, since the leaves dry quickly, but it is something to be aware of, especially if you already have disease issues in your garden.

The main downsides to drip irrigation are the added expense and time associated with setting it up. Also, with tightly planted crops, such as loose-leaf greens, it may be impractical to have enough drip lines to keep the whole bed evenly watered.

Fig. 3
Drip Irrigation for Tomatoes

Fig. 4
Drip Irrigation Next to Basil

Watering by Hand

Watering by hand, whether with a watering can or hose, is by far the most time-consuming irrigation technique, but that may not be a problem for some gardeners. If your soil has a high clay content it can be difficult to get the water to fully penetrate the soil. When watering clay soil by hand it is helpful to water one section until the water is just

beginning to pool at the surface, then do the same in another section. After watering the second sections, return to that first section which will have at this point absorbed any excess water and be ready to be watered again. Repeat this process multiple times until the soil is fully and evening watered.

One of the benefits of hand watering is that you can give different amounts of water to different plants based on their needs. As previously stated, this is not necessary, but can be nice to do if you choose.

If you are using row cover you should take it off before watering. This is because, with hand watering, you distribute a relatively high volume of water over a short period of time, and the majority of water may run off the row cover instead of being absorbed through the fabric into the soil as happens with rainstorms and other types of irrigation.

Weed mat has a similar issue to row cover, in that while weed mat is permeable to water, it can't absorb water at high volumes. And since it's impractical to remove weed mat in between hand waterings, it's preferable to either set up drip irrigation or use a sprinkler. It can be more challenging, but you can also very carefully hand water the plants through the holes in the fabric in which the plants are being grown through.

Fig. 5 Hand Watering

Deep Waterings

However you choose to irrigate your garden, it's important to give the soil deep saturating waterings. Plants will be much happier with infrequent deep waterings than daily light waterings.

Weed Mat and Mulch

Both weed mat and mulch help keep your soil from drying out. By putting a layer of material in between the soil and the dry air and sun, the soil retains moisture much longer. Weed mat does a better job of this than mulch, but mulch can still be very effective.

See pages 263-266 for instructions on setting up your weed mat and mulch.

Sidebar 1
Effects of Intense Sunlight on Vegetables

Row Cover

Row cover keeps the soil moist in a similar way as weed mat and mulch, but also has the added benefit of keeping the air around plants more humid, which most plants love. Row cover can also be used in conjunction with weed mat and/or mulch. Together they create an ideal environment for most vegetables to grow.

See page 258 for instructions on setting up your row cover.

Generally, at high altitudes there is no shortage of sun. While storms can pass by with great intensity, often the moment the storm is over, the sun comes right back out. Nine times out of ten this is a good thing. After all, sunlight is the main ingredient in photosynthesis, the primary process for plant growth.

However, the intensity of the high altitude sun can be challenging for a plant that isn't acclimated to it, and can cause the plant's leaves to burn and can even kill them. This most often occurs when moving a potted plant from a protected nursery, greenhouse or windowsill into the garden to be transplanted. The best way to avoid this is to place the plants in the shade of a tree or building for 3-7 days before transplanting, to slowly transition the plants to their new environment. If you choose to transplant your plants immediately upon getting them from a nursery, covering them afterwards with row cover helps their transition.

Crop Choice

Drought-Tolerant Plants

With a little care and irrigation, almost every type of vegetable can grow well in arid climates. That said, there are some vegetables that have an easier time than others. Table 1 shows a list of vegetables with low water needs.

Beyond the vegetables in Table 1, there can be differences in drought tolerance between varieties of the same plant. When choosing your seeds, read the descriptions and look for the term "drought tolerant".

Leaf Canopy

When plants mature, they create a canopy with their leaves that creates shade over the soil. This will keep the soil moist for longer. Plants with big sprawling leaves, like kale, have more of this effect than plants with fewer, thinner leaves, like onions. This shading effect will be most effective when the plants are fully grown, therefore more irrigation is needed when they are young.

Table 1
Drought Tolerant Plants

Beets
Beans
Asparagus
Perennial Herbs
Asian and Mustard Greens
Swiss Chard
Onion
Leeks
Garlic
Eggplant
Carrots
Parsnips

Fig. 6
Shade Canopy from Kale Leaves

Wind 5

At high elevations, you are more likely to experience high-speed destructive winds. While wind will probably not kill your garden plants, it can dry them out faster, blow away mulch, demolish fencing, and destroy row cover and weed mat. In this chapter you'll learn some simple techniques to minimize the detrimental effects of wind.

Windbreaks

Putting a physical object, or windbreak, in between the wind's path and your garden is the best way to keep your garden safe from wind. Many times, there is a predominant direction in which the wind travels in your area, and by knowing this direction you may only need to create a windbreak on one side of the garden. From experience, you may already know what direction that is, and if not, you can look for wind damaged plants (fig. 1) or keep an eye on the weather for a few weeks to get an idea.

Buildings

Placing your garden near a building can provide some of the most effective wind protection. The main concern with growing near a building is ensuring the garden gets enough sunlight. Your garden will get the most sun when located on the south side of the building.

An added benefit to growing near a building is the warmth the heated building emits (see page 12).

Living Windbreaks

You can also plant trees or shrubs in or near your garden that act as a windbreak. However, depending on their size when planted, it may take a few years of growth before they effectively block the wind.

One benefit of using ornamental or native plants as windbreaks is that you should be able to select a variety that is cold hardy, needs minimal watering and won't be of interest to animals.

Fig. 1
Wind-blown
Tree

Fence Windbreaks

If you already have a mesh open air fence around your garden it will be relatively easy to retrofit it to function as a windbreak. All you need to do is attach some fabric to the fence such as a weed mat, tarp, or windscreen. For this to work you need to make sure the fence is sturdy enough to withstand the added wind force. If you are concerned about the sturdiness of the fence, you can cut holes in the fabric, so some wind passes through, and/or only put the fabric on the bottom four feet of the fence.

Fig. 2
Peas
Growing up
a Fence to
Create a
Windbreak

Another option is to use the fence as a trellis and grow a vining plant on it. You can use a vegetable producing plant like peas, beans or cucumbers, or use an ornamental perennial. Hops is a great low maintenance perennial option for cold dry climates, especially if you like brewing beer.

Row Cover

Row cover is a great tool for protecting your plants from wind. The challenge with row cover is keeping it from blowing away. If the wind catches under the row cover it can act like a sail and go flying. At times of high winds, make sure your row cover is properly weighed down or else you may end up collecting it from your neighbor's roof.

See page 258 for instructions on setting up your row cover.

Wind Resistant Material

Whether you use a windbreak or not, it is advisable to use products in the garden that are less likely to blow away or get destroyed. This means building a sturdy fence, properly weighing down your row cover, and using heavier mulches like thick wood chips instead of hay or leaves. However you design your garden, make sure you ask yourself if what you're creating can withstand the windiest days in your climate.

Weeds 6

Dealing with unwanted weeds may be the most widespread challenge facing gardeners around the world. It doesn't matter if you're high in the mountains or on a tropical coast: if you have a garden, you will have weeds. Weeds in a garden can steal vital nutrients from the soil, decrease air circulation between plants, shade plants from the sun, act as hosts for pests and diseases, and overcrowd and therefore stunt plant growth. Weeds may not be something you ever completely get rid of in your garden, but with some care they can go from being a destructive garden presence to something altogether minor and manageable.

What Is a Weed?

A weed is any plant in your garden that you didn't plant and don't want to have growing. The majority of the time weeds are native plants that naturally grow in your area and have simply found their way into your garden. However, weeds can also be the unwanted offspring of the previous year's garden vegetables.

An example of your own vegetables becoming weeds would be if a tomato or squash, with their many seeds, was left on the ground at the end of the season, and the following year one of those seeds began to grow in an area where you were now growing another crop. If you never intended to grow that tomato or squash plant, and you don't want it growing there, then it is a weed.

Weeding

How Often to Weed

The fewer weeds in a garden, the happier your plants will be. This does not mean you need to be so meticulous that there is never a single weed growing, however, within the limits of your schedule and interest level, try to get rid of as many weeds as possible. Your weeding schedule is very specific to you and your garden, but as a general rule, give your garden a good weeding every week or two and/or try to remove weeds before they are larger than four inches.

> The most important rule of weeding is never let a weed produce seeds. A single weed can produce well over 100,000 seeds, so letting just one plant go to seed can be devastating for a garden. Your gardening life will be immensely more enjoyable if you adopt this rule. All other weeding methods and guidelines are secondary to this.

There are a few additional considerations when weeding:

- If a specific weed is beginning to produce seeds it is very important to remove it. As mentioned in the sidebar, a single garden weed can produce well over 100,000 seeds. Therefore, if you let one plant go to seed, you may be battling that weed's offspring for the next few years.

- If a weed has gotten so large that it is casting a shadow on your vegetables or overcrowding them so much that they can't grow as large as they'd like, it is very important to remove that weed.

- If there are perennial weeds (weeds that can survive for multiple years) growing in your garden it is important to remove them early, even if they aren't producing seeds or overly intruding on your other plants. This is necessary because if left unattended they will grow and expand from year to year and may eventually take over large areas of your garden. The most common perennial garden weed is grass. Like most perennial weeds, in order to kill grass organically you must pull or dig up their roots. Pulling and digging up perennial weeds will become more challenging as they get bigger, so get them early.

Fig. 1 Hand Pulling Weeds

- If you have concerns of a current or future pest or disease outbreak in your garden, you should be extra vigilant to keep your garden weed-free. Weeds can act as host plants for pests and diseases that then spread to your garden plants. As well, weeds, especially when large, diminish air circulation between your plants, which can encourage pests and diseases.

How to Weed a Garden

There is no wrong way to weed a garden, however the two most efficient methods are with a hoe and by hand. A mix of both methods will yield the best results.

Lightly agitating the top inch of soil around your plants with a hoe is a great way to kill young weeds. This method can even kill recently germinated weeds before they're even visible above the soil. Even if it doesn't look like there are many weeds in your garden, a quick weekly hoeing stops weeds before they become large and established.

Once a weed has an established root system and is at least 2-3 inches tall, hand pulling becomes the preferred method of weeding. If you hoe the garden regularly, there should only be a few weeds that need to be pulled. At this stage, be sure to pull the roots up along with the stem and leaves, since many weeds survive and regrow from just their roots.

Don't Give Your Weeds a Head Start

Native weeds evolved to live in your area and are therefore likely to be better suited to thrive in your climate than the non-native vegetables you are trying to grow. This means if left unattended, most weeds will grow faster and outcompete the other plants in your garden. Given that weeds already have this advantage, you don't want to give them a head start by seeding your vegetables into a weedy garden bed. Therefore, always weed your garden immediately before planting.

When preparing your garden beds for planting, if you normally till the soil with a shovel or rototiller (see tillage p. 33), then this already functions as that initial weeding. However, if you use a no-till method or it has been more than a few days in between tilling and the intended planting, than you first need to hand pull or gently hoe any weeds that are present.

Fig. 2 A Well Weeded Bed That's Ready for Planting

Weed Mat and Mulch

Another option, instead of actively weeding your garden, is to passively discourage them from growing. This is best done by using a weed mat or a thick layer of mulch to create a barrier between the soil and the air above. Generally, weed mat is more effective than mulch as a weed barrier, but mulch can certainly work well if you use a thick, 3 inch layer. This thick layer will that stops weeds from maneuvering their way through it.

Refer to pages 263-266 to learn how to set up your weed mat and mulch.

Fig. 3 Garden Beds Mulched with Hay

The Weed Seed Bank

The weed seed bank is a term to describe the many weed seeds that can stay viable in your soil for years before germinating. These seeds are waiting for the perfect combination of water, temperature and sometimes sunlight before germination is triggered. The weed seed bank is the reason that even if you meticulously weed your garden one year and don't let a single weed go to seed, the next year there still may be new weeds that germinate. The good news is that every year that you weed your garden and don't let any new weeds produce seeds, you diminish the weed seed band. And even though some weed seeds can survive in the soil for decades, for the most part, after five years the vast majority will have either germinated or will no longer be viable. While for the first few years it may be discouraging to weed your garden every year just to have a seemingly endless supply of weeds return the following year, if you stay vigilant, within 5 years you can deplete the weed seed bank and have a relatively weed-free garden.

Remember, even in the best of circumstances there are still weed seeds that can blow in with the wind, or be unintentionally carried in by an animal or gardener. Weeding goes hand in hand with being a gardener, but there is no reason it has to be an overly time-consuming task.

Fig. 4
Dandelion Seeds Blowing in the Wind

Soil 7

Very few soils are naturally the ideal growing medium for vegetables. Almost all soils have at least some deficiencies. But whether your soil is lacking in nutrients, has low organic matter, a high or low pH, or disproportionate amounts of sand or clay, there are always ways to adjust your soil and create a more productive garden.

The first thing to know is that your garden soil does not need to be perfect. Plants want to survive even more than you want them to. They will find a way. Never believe that your soil is too poor to have a garden. Even if you don't amend your soil in any way, your plants will still grow. However, with that said, a few simple amendments to the soil makes a world of difference in terms of the health and productivity of your plants.

But before you can fix a soil problem, you must identify it. Refer to page 12 to read about soil classification and testing. Know that improving your soil will be much easier if you submitted a soil test and received a soil report. You should get a soil report at least once every three years, but it is ideal to get it tested every year.

Nutrient Deficiency

Nitrogen (N), Phosphorus (P) and Potassium (K) are the three most necessary nutrients for plant growth. As plants grow, they absorb these nutrients from the soil, and when we harvest plant material to eat, we remove some of those nutrients from the garden, which over time causes nutrient deficiency.

Refer to your soil report to learn your current nutrient levels, and the quantity of those nutrients that should be added to reach optimal soil health.

Fig. 1 Healthy Plants are Given the Right Amount of Nutrients

Organic Fertilizer

Fertilizer is essentially a concentrated form of macronutrients (N-P-K) and it is one of the easiest and most effective ways to put nutrients back into the soil. But be aware, given how concentrated fertilizer is, it is easy to over apply, which does real harm to your soil and potentially makes it unsuitable for plant growth. For this reason, you must be very careful and follow the instructions of your soil report. However, if you did not get a soil report you can still use fertilizer, just follow the directions on the fertilizer packaging and know that without that soil report you are just guessing and may not be giving the soil everything it needs.

All fertilizer products have an N-P-K number on their packaging that tells you the percentage of the fertilizer that is pure nitrogen, pure phosphorus and pure potassium. When choosing a fertilizer also keep in mind how quickly the nutrients from the fertilizer will be available to the plants. Nutrients from most fertilizers are available immediately, however some may take up to two weeks or occasionally all season before being available to the plants.

Applying Fertilizer: The easiest, least time-consuming method is to simply apply a fertilizer once per year to your garden beds before planting. This is done by applying the appropriate quantity of fertilizer to the beds as stated on your soil report and then mixing it into the top 3-4 inches of soil before planting.

While this method alone is sufficient and produces happy plants, most full season crops prefer additional fertilizer applications throughout the growing season. This method is called *sidedressing.* When giving the initial fertilizer application at the beginning of the season it is best to refer to your soil report, however when sidedressing, your fertilizer choice can be a bit more simplified. In general, you can use a high nitrogen fertilizer (e.g. 5-0-0) for leaf harvested plants like kale or chard, and an equal ratio N-P-K premixed fertilizer (e.g. 5-5-5) for all other vegetables. Refer to Table 1 for sidedressing specifics and notable exceptions.

Because of plant root growth you can't mix in the sidedressed fertilizer to the same depth as the first spring

Fig. 2
Organic
Fertilizer

• *Premixed Fertilizer:* This is the most common form of fertilizer. Its nutrients are quickly available to plants and frequently have a base of dehydrated manure with other ingredients added. Premixed fertilizers can have varying N-P-K levels but frequently measure around 5-5-5. Unfortunately, many times these fertilizers falsely advertise those N-P-K levels as ideal for your soil in all situations, when in reality, the nutrient needs of your soil are unique to your garden and what you're growing. With a soil report and some understanding of your garden you won't fall for this trap and will know when a premixed fertilizer's N-P-K rating is and is not what your soil needs.

• *Blood Meal:* Blood meal has fast nutrient availability, and an N-P-K of 12-0-0. It is a great amendment if you find that your garden needs nitrogen but has sufficient levels of phosphorus and potassium.

• *Bone Meal:* Bone meal has slow availability with an N-P-K of 2-14-0. It is a great amendment if you need phosphorus but not much nitrogen or potassium. Because of its slow release, one application in the spring is sufficient for the whole season. Be cautious when using in alkaline soil since a recent study suggests that the phosphorus in bone meal may only be available to soils with a pH below 7.0.

• *Fish Meal:* This quick available dry fertilizer typically has an N-P-K of 10-5-0. This is an excellent fertilizer when its N-P-K matches your soil's needs. The main downside is it smells a bit fishy.

• *Fish Emulsion:* Unlike fish meal that is a dry fertilizer, fish emulsion is liquid. It has an N-P-K of 9-0-0 and unfortunately has a very potent fish odor that far surpasses that of fish meal. This is a great nitrogen fertilizer, but don't underestimate its odor.

• *Kelp Meal:* This has fast nutrient availability with an N-P-K of 1-0-2. It is a good choice when your soil primarily needs potassium (K). Kelp meal can sometimes be difficult to find at a nursery, so it may need to be ordered online.

There are many other types of fertilizer that may be available at your nursery. They include bat guano, soybean meal, corn meal, cotton seed meal, and alfalfa meal. They all have unique N-P-K ratings and may be just what your garden needs.

There is no one-size-fits-all fertilizer. The right fertilizer for you depends on your soil's needs, the time of year you apply it, what's available at your garden store, as well as your general preference.

fertilizer application. Instead, if it is a granular or powdered fertilizer, mix it into the top inch of the soil 4 inches away from the plant's stem. If it is a liquid fertilizer, appropriately dilute it in a watering can (as per the fertilizer's instructions) and water the plant's roots.

Compost

The best benefit of compost is the organic matter it provides for the soil, however it also adds some nutrients as well. The exact amount of nutrients compost provides varies greatly depending on what was composted and how. That said, typical compost has an N-P-K around .5-.5-.5. While .5-.5-.5 is relatively modest compared to some fertilizers, it still plays a beneficial role in plant growth, especially since you'll apply it in larger quantities than fertilizer. If your sole need is to increase nutrients in your soil, fertilizer is the best option, but if you're already adding compost to increase the organic matter in your soil, you won't need to add quite as much fertilizer to reach the intended nutrient levels.

Fig. 3 Potatoes like to be Sidedressed One Month After they Emerge from the Soil

Table 1
Sidedressing for Common Garden Vegetables

Fertilize at a quantity of 1 tablespoon per small plant (under 12 inches tall) and 2 tablespoons per large plant (over 12 inches tall). This is assuming fertilizer N-P-K values around 5-5-5 (for equal N-P-K ratio fertilizer) or 5-0-0 (for high nitrogen fertilizer). If your fertilizer N-P-K values are higher or lower, adjust the fertilizer quantity.

	Times Per Season	Timing	Fertilizer Type
Asparagus	2	In the spring after the harvest period, and again in the fall	Equal N-P-K ratio fertilizer
Basil	Not necessary		
Beans	Not necessary		
Beets	1	When plants are 4-5 inches tall	Equal N-P-K ratio fertilizer
Bok Choi	1	One month after planting	High Nitrogen Fertilizer
Broccoli	2	Three weeks after transplanting, and 6 weeks after transplanting	High Nitrogen Fertilizer for first sidedressing and equal N-P-K ratio fertilizer for second sidedressing
Brussels Sprouts	2	One month after transplanting, and two months after transplanting	High Nitrogen Fertilizer for first sidedressing and equal N-P-K ratio fertilizer for second sidedressing
Cabbage	2	Three weeks after transplanting, and 6 weeks after transplanting	High Nitrogen Fertilizer for first sidedressing and equal N-P-K ratio fertilizer for second sidedressing

Table 1
Sidedressing for Common Garden Vegetables (continued)

	Times Per Season	Timing	Fertilizer Type
Cabbage, Napa	2	Three weeks after transplanting, and 6 weeks after transplanting	High Nitrogen Fertilizer for first sidedressing and equal N-P-K ratio fertilizer for second sidedressing
Carrots	1	6 weeks after germination	Equal N-P-K ratio fertilizer
Cauliflower	2	One month after transplanting, and two months after transplanting	High Nitrogen Fertilizer for first sidedressing and equal N-P-K ratio fertilizer for second sidedressing
Chives	Not necessary		
Cilantro	Not necessary		
Corn, Sweet	2	When plants are 8 inches tall, and again when silks first appear	Equal N-P-K ratio fertilizer
Cucumber	2-3	When plants begin to vine, and again when flowers first appear. Fertilize a third time a month after flowers first appear if the plant is still healthy and producing	Equal N-P-K ratio fertilizer

73

Table 1
Sidedressing for Common Garden Vegetables (continued)

	Times Per Season	Timing	Fertilizer Type
Dill	Not necessary		
Eggplant	1	When fruits first appear	Equal N-P-K ratio fertilizer, or high Phosphorus fertilizer
Garlic	Not necessary		
Kale/Collards	3	One month, two months and three months after transplanting	High Nitrogen Fertilizer
Kohlrabi	1	One month after transplanting	Equal N-P-K ratio fertilizer
Lavender	Not necessary		
Leeks	3	When plants are 8 inches tall, again a month after, and again a month after that	Equal N-P-K ratio fertilizer
Lettuce	1	After first harvest for loose leaf, or 3 weeks after germination for head lettuce	High Nitrogen fertilizer

Table 1
Sidedressing for Common Garden Vegetables (continued)

	Times Per Season	Timing	Fertilizer Type
Melons	2-3	When plants begin to vine, again when flowers first appear, and again a month after that.	Equal N-P-K ratio fertilizer
Mustard and Asian Greens	1	After first harvest	High Nitrogen fertilizer
Onion	2	When plants are 6-8 inches tall, and again when bulbs start to form	Equal N-P-K ratio fertilizer
Oregano	Not necessary		
Parsley	2	One month after transplanting, and again a month after that	High Nitrogen fertilizer
Parsnips	2	6 weeks after germination, and again a month after that	Equal N-P-K ratio fertilizer
Peas	Not necessary		
Pepper	2	One month after transplanting, and again a month after that	Equal N-P-K ratio fertilizer
Potato	1	One month after plants emerge from soil	Equal N-P-K ratio fertilizer

Table 1
Sidedressing for Common Garden Vegetables (continued)

	Times Per Season	Timing	Fertilizer Type
Radish, Turnips, Rutabaga	1	One month after transplanting	Equal N-P-K ratio fertilizer
Rosemary	Not necessary		
Spinach	1	One month after planting	High Nitrogen fertilizer
Summer Squash and Zucchini	2-3	When plants begin to vine, and again when flowers first appear. Fertilize a third time a month after flowers first appear if the plant is still healthy and producing	Equal N-P-K ratio fertilizer
Sweet Potatoes	Not necessary		
Swiss Chard	2	One month after transplanting, and again a month after that	High Nitrogen fertilizer
Thyme	Not necessary		
Tomatoes	2	One month after transplanting, and again when fruits begin to form	Low Nitrogen fertilizer
Winter Squash	2	When plants begin to vine, and again when flowers first appear.	Equal N-P-K ratio fertilizer

Sidebar 2
Converting Your Soil Report's Nutrient Recommendations to Actual Fertilizer

The most user-friendly soil reports give their fertilizer recommendations based on the amount of a specific N-P-K fertilizer needed. They may say something like "apply 6 pounds of a 5-5-5 fertilizer per 100 square feet". But sometimes, instead of giving a fertilizer recommendation, soil reports give their recommendations as the number of pounds of a certain nutrient that is needed per 100 square feet. The issue with this is that no fertilizer is 100% of any specific nutrient. If a bag of fertilizer has an N-P-K ratio of 5-5-5, what that means is that 5% of that fertilizer is pure nitrogen, 5% is pure phosphorus, and 5% is pure potassium. Therefore, if your soil report give a nutrient recommendation rather than a fertilizer recommendation you must use the below formula to calculate your specific fertilizer needs.

$$\left(\begin{array}{c}\text{pounds of pure}\\\text{nutrients needed}\\\text{for 100 sq. ft.}\end{array}\right) \div \left(\begin{array}{c}\text{percentage}\\\text{of nutrient}\\\text{in fertilizer}\end{array}\right) = \left(\begin{array}{c}\text{pounds of}\\\text{fertilizer needed}\\\text{for 100 sq. ft.}\end{array}\right)$$

For example, if your soil report says you need 0.3 pounds of nitrogen per 100 square feet, and the fertilizer you are using has an N value of 5 (aka 5% or .05), then your equation would look like this:

$$\left(\begin{array}{c}\text{pounds of pure}\\\text{nutrients needed}\\\text{for 100 sq. ft.}\end{array}\right) \div \left(\begin{array}{c}\text{percentage}\\\text{of nutrient}\\\text{in fertilizer}\end{array}\right) = \left(\begin{array}{c}\text{pounds of}\\\text{fertilizer needed}\\\text{for 100 sq. ft.}\end{array}\right)$$

$$\left(\,0.3\,\right) \div \left(\,.05\,\right) = \left(\,6\,\right)$$

And if your garden isn't exactly 100 square feet use the below formula to convert the value:

$$\left(\begin{array}{c}\text{pounds of} \\ \text{fertilizer needed} \\ \text{for 100 sq.ft.}\end{array}\right) \div \left(\text{100 sq.ft}\right) \times \left(\begin{array}{c}\text{actual} \\ \text{garden} \\ \text{sq.ft.}\end{array}\right) = \left(\begin{array}{c}\text{pounds of fertilizer} \\ \text{needed per actual} \\ \text{garden sq.ft.}\end{array}\right)$$

To continue the example, if you need 6 pounds of fertilizer per 100 square feet, but your garden is 80 square feet, your equation would look like this:

$$\left(\begin{array}{c}\text{pounds of} \\ \text{fertilizer needed} \\ \text{for 100 sq.ft.}\end{array}\right) \div \left(\text{100 sq.ft}\right) \times \left(\begin{array}{c}\text{actual} \\ \text{garden} \\ \text{sq.ft.}\end{array}\right) = \left(\begin{array}{c}\text{pounds of fertilizer} \\ \text{needed per actual} \\ \text{garden sq.ft.}\end{array}\right)$$

$$\left(\ 6\ \right) \div \left(\ 100\ \right) \times \left(\ 80\ \right) = \left(\ 4.8\ \right)$$

Keep in mind that you have to convert the soil report's recommendations for each N, P and K value separately. And after doing so you may find that the amount of each nutrient needed does not neatly match up to the N-P-K ratio of a single store bought bag of fertilizer. If that is the case, you need to mix and match multiple fertilizers to reach that intended ratio of N,P and K.

Organic Matter

Organic matter improves soil structure, enhances water drainage, feeds beneficial microorganisms and insects, and provides nutrients to the plants at a healthy rate. Refer to your soil report to learn your soil's organic matter percentage. The healthiest garden soils have a range of 3-8% organic matter.

Organic matter naturally decreases over time if you are removing plant material from the garden and not replacing it. *Sidebar 3* Improving and maintaining healthy organic matter levels is not *The Organic* something you do once and forget about, but instead is best *Matter* thought of as a gradual, yearly project. The two best ways to add *Cycle of the Garden Ecosystem*

Organic matter naturally decreases over time as microorganisms slowly break it down. While this process is natural and healthy since it turns organic matter into a material that plants can draw nutrients from, it still depletes the organic matter that would otherwise enhance water drainage and improve soil structure. In balanced, closed systems, like forests or prairies, the organic matter broken down by microorganisms is replenished by new organic matter from recently dead plant material. However, when gardening, you interrupt that closed system when you remove plant material from the garden in the form of food to eat. Unless you regularly add organic matter back into the soil, it gradually becomes more and more depleted.

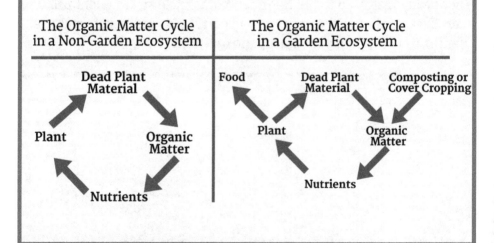

The Organic Matter Cycle in a Non-Garden Ecosystem

The Organic Matter Cycle in a Garden Ecosystem

organic matter to the soil are through adding compost or cover cropping.

Compost

Compost, which is decomposed and aged plant and/or animal material, is a great amendment to your soil if you want to add organic matter. By creating your own compost at home, you will know exactly what is in it, but buying bags from a nursery can be just as healthy for your soil.

The best time to add compost is in the spring before planting, or in the fall after you're done harvesting. In general, it is good to add 1-3 inches of compost to the soil every year and mix it into the soil to a depth of 6-8 inches using a shovel, pitchfork or rototiller. If you add more than 3 inches of compost you risk adding salts or nutrients into the soil at a concentrated level that can be unhealthy for plants (especially if there's manure in your compost). As well, if you add more than 3 inches at a time you may have difficulty incorporating it into the soil down to that 6-8 inch depth. Adding 1-3 inches of compost is unlikely to increase the soil's organic matter content more than

Sidebar 4
Types of
Compost

• *Plant Material:* Composted plant material frequently consists of vegetable scraps, yard waste and/or wood chips.

• *Animal Material:* Animal compost, also called manure, most frequently comes from chicken or cow excrement. Manure generally has a higher N-P-K value than plant-based compost, but it also risks having unhealthy levels of salts, especially if it is not aged long enough.

• *Earthworm Castings:* While traditional compost is organic material that has been primarily eaten by microorganisms, earthworm castings are organic material that has been eaten and excreted by earthworms. Earthworm compost is generally the highest quality compost, but also the most expensive. An at-home earthworm bin is a fun small-scale way of creating your own excellent compost at home.

1%, so if your soil needs more than a 1% increase in organic matter it may take a few years to reach an ideal level.

Whereas with fertilizer you'll want to be as exact as possible with how much you apply, when adding compost, you can be a little less precise. If you don't add quite enough *Fig. 4* compost one year your plants will be fine, and if you add a bit *Vegetable Scraps* too much (as long as you're able to work it into the soil) your *Ready to be* plants will also be fine. *Composted*

Cover Crops

Cover cropping is when you densely plant a crop in an area, but instead of harvesting anything from the plant, you incorporate the plant's biomass back into the soil. Cover cropping works by taking water, energy from the sun, and ingredients from the soil and creating new organic matter in the form of leaves, stems and roots. And when you mix that organic matter into the soil and let it decompose, you raise the organic matter content of your soil. Sometimes cover crops are also used to prevent an otherwise bare piece of earth from eroding or being overtaken by weeds.

Cover cropping is a popular technique with farmers, and in recent years more gardeners have started using this method.

While it may be appealing to use this technique instead of applying compost, there are a few concerns to consider.

The main question is whether you want to devote part of your garden to growing a plant that won't produce food. If you have a lot of extra space in your garden this may not be a concern, however for many gardeners every square foot is precious and taking some of it out of production may not be appealing. One situation where this may not be a problem is when planting a fall cover crop after your summer plants are done for the season.

Fig. 5
Field of Oats

Another concern is how you incorporate the cover crop into the soil when it's fully grown. Many cover crops are perennials even in cold climates, meaning they survive the winter and continue growing in the spring. This means that come spring, before you can plant your veggies, you will need to kill the cover crops. Without a solid plan to manage your cover

Table 2
Common
Cover Crops

	Planting Time	Perennial/ Annual	Adds Nitrogen
Rye	Fall	Perennial	No
Oats	Fall	Annual	No
Vetch	Mid-Late Summer	Perennial	Yes
Clover	Late Summer	Perennial	Yes
Peas	Spring-Summer	Annual	Yes
Buckwheat	Late Spring-Early Summer	Annual	No

crops, they risk becoming hard to kill weeds. If you own a rototiller this may not be a problem, but if you are weeding and turning the soil with hand tools then this can be a big project. The best solution for this challenge is to grow annual cover crops that die in the winter. Then all you need to do come spring is gently incorporate the dead plant material back into the soil.

Cover cropping can be a great technique as long as you have the space and time to grow them, and a solid understanding of their life cycle. If you want to try cover cropping, oats can be a great plant to start with. Oats are fast growing and moderately frost tolerant, however hard winter frosts will ultimately kill them. After they die, they leave a nice mat of plant material that holds the soil in place through the winter and is easily incorporated into the soil come spring.

High or Low pH

PH is the measure of your soil's acidity or alkalinity. Its scale ranges from 0-14, with zero being the most acidic, 14 the most alkaline, and 7 being neutral. While most plants prefer a soil pH within the range of 6-7.5, that does not mean you can't grow healthy and productive plants outside of those ranges. Whenever possible it will be healthiest for your plants if you adjust the pH to their optimal range.

Adjusting for Soil Acidity

The easiest way to amend acidic soil is to add garden lime. Garden lime is ground limestone and is safe for your garden if used in the right quantity. Your soil report should tell you the appropriate application rate.

Garden lime has a slow release rate. While you may see beneficial results within the first season, it may take up to a year for the full effect. For this reason, it is best to apply it in the fall, so by the spring planting there has been at least a few months of time for the lime to take effect.

The alkalizing effects of lime slowly diminish over time. Therefore, you need to reapply lime roughly every 3 years.

Alkaline Soil

Generally, an overly alkaline soil is not all that bad for your garden. While your plants may have trouble absorbing certain nutrients from the soil, especially phosphorus, plants are much less affected by alkaline soil than acidic soil. This is good news because it is also very difficult to make an alkaline soil more acidic. Most high alkaline soils naturally contain limestone and making a soil more acidic when limestone is present is very difficult. If you have a high alkaline soil, the best advice is to ignore anyone that says it's a big problem. Just be careful to keep your soil nutrients at the right levels and if necessary, grow vegetables that are better suited for alkaline soil (see 'Ideal pH Ranges of Common Vegetables' p. 18).

Overly Sandy or Clayey Soils

Soils with disproportionate amounts of sand and clay tend to have poor soil structure, drainage issues, and unhealthy nutrient levels. While your soil's structure may initially seem like one of the least changeable aspects of your garden, in reality it can be improved like almost everything else in your garden.

Adding Compost to Improve Sand or Clay Soils

Whether your soil has too much clay or too much sand, adding compost is the best answer to both issues. Increasing organic matter in your soil by adding compost will help improve water retention and drainage as well as help the sand and clay particles to form aggregated

Fig. 6
Compost

clumps that further improve the soil's structure.

While adding compost is by far the best solution for clay and sandy soils, there are limits to how immediately effective it can be. It is very difficult to raise the organic matter more than 1% each year, and even that can be challenging. While you will see immediate results from adding a single amendment of compost, it may take years of incorporating compost to get the full results.

Fig. 7 Light Colored Soil Many Times Correlates to Low Organic Matter, Refer to Your Soil Report to be Sure

To amend compost to your soil, add 3 inches of it every year in the early spring before plants are in the ground, or in the fall after the garden is done for the season. Work the compost into the soil to a depth of 6-8 inches. While it may take years for your soil to have an ideal composition, after every yearly compost application you soil will significantly improve. And just because you don't have "perfect" soil doesn't mean you can't have an incredible garden. Most plants can still be healthy and productive even in a less than ideal soil.

Adding Sand to Improve Clay Soils

A less effective, yet still viable alternative to adding compost to clay soils, is to add sand. By adding sand, you can reduce the percentage of clay and create a more hospitable growing environment for plants. The benefit of adding sand instead of compost is that sand is cheap, and the effects are more permanent since in time, unlike sand, compost fully decomposes and needs reapplication.

The downside of adding sand is that a large amount of it is required to alter the soil's composition, and since store-bought sand has no nutrients or organic matter, you will essentially be diluting the nutrients and organic matter that are already present in the soil.

It is also very difficult to fully mix sand in with a clay soil. You may find that instead of completely mixing together, the sand simply coats the outside of larger clay clumps. While coating the clay clumps with sand will not truly alter the soil's composition, it will at least create passageways for air and water to travel through.

There may be situations where adding sand logistically makes more sense than adding compost, but typically, adding compost will more effectively improve clay soils.

Raised Beds for Clay Soils

One of the biggest challenges with overly clay soil is that it drains very slowly. This can stunt plant growth, and cause a meager harvest. One way to address this issue is to use raised beds (p. 261). By using raised beds water is less likely to lay stagnant in the soil since it will be above the natural soil level.

Fig. 8 Weed Mat Helps Retain Moisture for Squash Plants

As well, if you choose to fill your raised beds with

store-bought soil or potting mix, the plants will no longer be growing in clay soil (unless the roots grow past the depth of the raised bed into the natural clay soil beneath it).

Weed Mat and Row Cover for Sandy Soils

One of the difficulties with sandy soil is that it drains so fast that it can be difficult to provide enough water for your plants. This problem is exacerbated by the dry and windy climate of many high altitude areas. By using weed mat (p. 263) and/or row cover (p. 258) you can keep moisture in the soil for longer. While weed mat and row cover won't stop water from draining deeper into the earth than roots can access, they slow the process of evaporation, which in turn keeps moisture in the top section of the soil for longer.

Low Pollination 8

Some high altitude climates don't have sufficient insect populations to properly pollinate a vegetable garden. A low or non-existent pollinator population can result in plants that look healthy and have many flowers, yet produce little to no fruit. If you live in an area with a low pollinator population, and still want to grow plants that require insect pollination, there are a number of techniques you can use to ensure you have an abundant and fruitful garden.

Which Plants Need Pollinating?

Only plants from which you harvest their fruits require pollination. In a garden this includes beans, cucumbers, eggplants, melons, peas, peppers, summer squash/zucchini, tomatoes, and winter squash. However, not all plants that require pollination need insect pollinators. Some plants are pollinated by wind and others self-pollinate without any external influence (see table 1).

How Plants Are Pollinated

Pollination occurs when pollen from the male part of the flower (the anther) comes in contact with the female part of the flower (the stigma). There are multiple ways that a flower can be pollinated, but the most common are through insects and wind.

Insect pollination occurs when an insect physically takes pollen from the anther and brings it to the stigma. The most common pollinator insects are bees, however butterflies, moths, and some species of flies may also pollinate your garden. Plants in the cucurbit family (cucumbers, melons, and squash) rely entirely on insect pollination.

Wind pollination occurs when the pollen from the male anther is blown in the wind and then lands on the female stigma. Some plants, like corn, rely entirely on wind pollination, while others like eggplants, peppers, and tomatoes can be pollinated by either wind or insects.

Beans and peas are unique in that they can be pollinated by insects or wind, but do not require either. Pollination occurs reliably for these plants without any external factors.

Types of Flowers

Whether a plant requires insect or wind pollination depends on the type of flowers that plant produces.

Perfect Flowers

When a plant has both the male and female parts (anther and stigma) all within one flower then it is called a perfect

Table 1 Pollination Needs of Common Vegetables

Plants Requiring Insect Pollination	Cucumbers, Melons, Summer Squash/Zucchini, Winter Squash
Plants Requiring Wind Pollination	Corn
Plants Requiring Insect or Wind Pollination	Eggplants, Peppers, Tomatoes
Plants Not Requiring Any External Influence for Pollination	Beans, Peas
Plants that Don't Need Pollination	Asparagus, Beets, Bok Choi, Broccoli, Brussels Sprouts, Cabbage, Carrots, Cauliflower, Garlic, Herbs, Kale, Kohlrabi, Leek, Lettuce, Onions, Parsnips, Potatoes, Radishes, Rutabagas, Spinach, Sweet Potatoes, Swiss Chard, Turnips

flower. Perfect flowers can produce a fruit two different ways: they can be self-pollinated with pollen already present in the flower, or be cross-pollinated with pollen from another flower.

While cross-pollination is necessary for new genetic material to be incorporated, self-pollination is a valuable evolutionary tool that allows a plant to produce offspring even when conditions don't allow for cross-pollination.

However, while self-pollination occurs entirely within a single flower that does not mean pollination is guaranteed. The anther and stigma within a perfect flower are not physically touching, therefore pollen must somehow travel that short distance from the anther to the stigma.

Sidebar 1
Determining Pollinator Populations

There is no perfect way to determine if you have enough wild pollinators to successfully grow a plant. The best option may be to simply grow one or two plants and see how they do. If those plants grow well but don't produce much fruit, then there are likely not enough pollinators.

Another option is to ask a neighboring gardener what their experience has been growing plants that require pollination. If a neighbor's garden is within a mile of yours, you can comfortably assume you will have a similar pollinator population.

Fig. 1
Bee Pollinating Tomato Flower

For beans and peas, pollination most often occurs as the flower is opening and pollen naturally drops from the anther onto the stigma. For other perfect flowering crops like eggplants, peppers, and tomatoes, they most often require either insects or wind to help agitate the pollen off the anther and onto the stigma.

Imperfect Flowers

Unlike perfect flowers, imperfect flowers are either entirely male or female, and therefore contain either an anther or a stigma. Some imperfect flowers, like corn, are pollinated exclusively by wind, while others, like cucumbers, melons, and squash, are pollinated exclusively by insects. All common garden vegetables with imperfect flowers produce both male and female flowers on the same plant.

Table 2 List of Vegetables with Perfect and Imperfect Flowers

Perfect Flowers	Beans, Eggplant, Peas, Peppers, Tomatoes
Imperfect Flowers	Corn, Cucumbers, Melons, Summer Squash/Zucchini, Winter Squash

Growing Plants with Imperfect Flowers in Areas with Low Pollinator Populations

If you don't have sufficient wild pollinators in your area, yet you want to grow crops in the cucurbit family, like cucumbers, melons, summer squash/zucchini, or winter squash, you must employ at least one of the following techniques.

Grow Seedless Varieties

The easiest method for growing imperfect flowering crops without wild pollinators is to grow specific varieties that have been bred not to need pollination to produce a fruit. These varieties are called parthenocarpic, which means they don't require pollination and produce seedless fruits. Parthenocarpic varieties are not genetically modified, and their seeds can be purchased organically, like any other vegetable seed.

Unfortunately, not all vegetables have parthenocarpic seed varieties for sale. Currently the only widely available parthenocarpic vegetable seeds for sale are cucumbers and zucchini. Therefore, if you want to grow melons or winter squash, you will need to use an alternative method.

Hand Pollination

While it may be time intensive, hand pollinating imperfect flowers is a viable method for pollination.

The first step before hand pollination can occur is to determine which flowers are male and which are female. While male and female cucurbit flowers look similar, female flowers have small immature fruits growing directly behind the flower, even before pollination. They will also be growing on longer stems than male flowers, and will be growing as a single separate flower, whereas male flowers tend to grow in clusters of 3 to 5.

Fig. 2 Female Cucumber Flower with Immature Fruit Growing Behind It

Many cucurbit varieties produce a flush of male flowers before the first female flowers appear, so don't be discouraged if there are no female flowers for the first week or two of the flower stage.

Once you are comfortable with the difference between a male and a female flower, the next step is to physically transfer pollen from the male flower to the female flower. This can be done in two different ways. The first method is to cut the male flower from the plant and touch its anther to the female flower's stigma. You can use one male flower for multiple female flowers.

Another method for hand pollination is to take a cotton swab or small paint brush and touch it to the male flower's pollen and then transfer that pollen to the female flower's stigma.

Fig. 3 Female Squash Flower with Immature Fruit Growing Behind It

Raise Honey Bees

One way to solve your pollinator problems and get some honey in the process is to raise honey bees near your garden. Honeybees are excellent pollinators, and a single hive should solve any pollinator problems your garden may have.

Attract Wild Pollinators

While vegetable flowers produce plenty of tasty nectar for wild pollinators, they alone may not be sufficient to attract a large enough population of insects to your garden. If you have the space in your garden, you may consider growing other flowering plants that will help attract wild pollinators. The more flowers your garden has the more likely it is that pollinator insects will visit.

Sidebar 2
Just Don't
Grow Them

Be aware that if the pollinator population in your area is too low, no amount of aromatic and nectar-rich flowers will attract enough insects to properly pollinate your garden. If this is the case, you will need to use an alternative method.

If you don't have sufficient wild pollinators and you don't want to commit to any of the methods discussed in this chapter, another viable option is to simply not grow fruiting plants. There are many vegetables you can still grow that do not require pollination, like all root and leaf crops. Just because you choose not to grow tomatoes or cucumbers does not mean you can't have a full and vibrant garden.

Growing Plants with Perfect Flowers in Areas with Low Pollinator Populations

Since perfect flowers can be pollinated by wind, insects, or at times without any external influence, a low pollinator population will frequently not affect a plant's yields. While insects are necessary for cross-pollination, a gentle, normal wind is normally sufficient for self-pollination. Beans and peas are almost never affected by a low pollinator population, however when growing eggplants, peppers, or tomatoes you may notice a slight decrease in the pollination rate. This decrease will normally not significantly affect fruit yields, however if you feel it is, there are some options available to improve the self-pollination rate.

Some of the same methods used to improve imperfect flower pollination, like attracting wild pollinators with ornamental flowers or raising honey bees, will also work for perfect flowers. However, one of the easiest and most effective methods to influence perfect flower pollination is to shake or agitate the plant, which will mimic a gust of wind and cause pollination within the flower. The two easiest ways to do this are to physically shake the plant or place a vibrating electric toothbrush on a branch near the flowers. The best time to do this is midday, and should be done every 2 to 3 days during a plant's flowering stage.

Sidebar 3

Row Cover and Pollinators

Row cover has many benefits in a garden, but unfortunately this thin fabric that covers your plants can also act as a physical barrier for pollinator insects and wind. If you're growing vegetables that needs pollination you can still use row cover when they are young, but once they begin to produce flowers, pollination will be the most successful if the row cover is removed.

Growing parthenocarpic varieties or hand pollinating are still viable options if you want to grow vegetables under row cover throughout their flower stage. As well, if you are growing vegetables with perfect flowers, self-pollination by wind may still be possible under row cover, however unless the wind is very strong, the pollination rate may be reduced.

Wildlife 9

Keeping your plants safe from hungry critters can feel like a daunting task. This is especially true at high elevations where, with less natural vegetation, animals are especially motivated to access your garden. As well, higher elevations tend to be less populated by humans, and where there are less people there tends to be more wildlife. There are a few simple and not-so-simple techniques you can employ to ensure your plants stay safe from deer, rodents, rabbits, birds and any other wild visitors you may have.

Identifying the Culprit

Before you determine how to stop an animal from eating your plants, you must first identify it. If you haven't caught the animal in the act, sometimes it can be challenging to know which animal is to blame.

Deer

Deer attack the above-ground portions of many garden plants. One of the easiest ways to spot a deer's presence is to look for their tracks around the damaged plants.

Because deer are so large, they are more likely than other animals to eat larger plant stems along with leaves. The damage may look like they gave an undiscerning haircut to the plant. Deer will also leave jagged markings on the left-over parts of the plant. These markings come from deer ripping the plant material from the plant rather than making distinct bites like other animals do.

Rodents

Rodents tend to prefer root crops over leafy greens, but that certainly won't stop them from eating your lettuce if nothing better is around. If you find one or two bites taken out of every plant in an area, this is frequently done by rodents. Most rodents can be identified by the burrows they leave behind.

Mice have the smallest burrow hole, normally only 1 inch in diameter. Chipmunks have a burrow size of 2 inches. Ground squirrels and prairie dogs have a burrow size of 4 inches. And groundhogs (also known as woodchucks) have very large burrows, around 6-8 inches. While tree squirrels and raccoons may do some light burrowing, they won't have the same intricate tunnels as other rodents.

While it may be hard to identify exactly which type of rodent is damaging your garden, the most important information for managing them is to identify if they are burrowing rodents or not and the approximate size of the rodent, which can be gleaned from their burrow holes.

Fig. 1 Mouse Nibbling on a Celeriac

Rabbits

Rabbits eat the leaves, stems and roots of many garden plants. Unlike the jagged rips of deer damage, rabbits make a clean cut with their teeth. Their damage is also limited by their height and is rarely more than two feet above the ground. They also frequently leave their small round droppings near the plants they have eaten.

Fig. 2
Deer Tracks

Birds

Birds have a tendency to eat newly planted seeds, young seedlings (especially corn and peas) and ripe juicy fruits (such as tomatoes and melons). Look for peck marks in the fruiting vegetables, as well as their footprints in the dirt as they scratch up the earth looking for seeds and insects.

By eating harmful insects and weed seeds, birds can also benefit a garden. Just because you see birds in your garden doesn't mean they are a problem. Only take steps to get rid of them if they start to damage your plants.

Protecting Your Garden

Once you know the animals you need to protect your garden from, you can take the necessary steps to do so. There are many ways to protect your garden, and you may find that the best option is a combination of techniques.

Fencing (for deer, rodents and rabbits)

A fence is the most obvious and generally the most effective way of keeping non-flying animals out of your garden.

And while a well-made fence can be a demanding project, it may be necessary in certain situations. The type of fence you put up depends on the type of animals you are trying to keep out. You may need to combine multiple fencing strategies to provide protection from more than one type of animal.

Deer-Proof Fencing: Deer can be devastating to a garden. They are voracious eaters, and given that they can jump eight feet high, it is a significant project keeping them out. There are however several fencing methods you can use.

- The most straightforward type of deer-proof fence is an eight-foot-high mesh netting fence secured with metal or wood corner posts. While constructing this type of fence is no small project, it is the most effective way of keeping deer out.

- An alternative to constructing an eight-foot-tall vertical fence is to set up a six-foot-tall fence that slants outward at a 45° angle. Deer can jump high, but not both high and far. With this type of fence, deer will try, and fail, to walk under it. This design can save you a couple of feet of fence height, but creating a 45° angle fence will be a slightly more challenging construction project.

Fig. 3 This fence may look nice, but in reality it will only lightly deter deer, rodents and rabbits

- A 4 to 5 foot tall solid picket fence can also be effective. While a deer could potentially jump over this fence, they don't like to jump over an object if they can't see what is on the other side. And even if they'd be interested in eating your garden plants, if they can't see through the fence, they likely won't know the plants are there. This style of fence can feel a lot less daunting to construct than an eight-foot-tall fence, however deer may eventually learn that it's safe to jump over it, and even a single deer visit can be destructive to a garden. As well, this type of fence may cast shade into your garden, which most plants won't appreciate.

- An interesting modification to the single 4 to 5 foot fence technique is instead to use two 4 to 5 foot fences roughly five feet apart from each other around the perimeter of the garden. Deer have poor depth perception and don't like to be trapped in small spaces, therefore they are unlikely to try jumping over that first fence. For this technique the outer fence should be mesh and transparent, and the inner fence can either be mesh or a solid material.

- Electric fencing can be very effective, and can be powered through a solar panel or from an outlet. If deer interest in your garden is low, you may be able to get by with a single strand 30 inches above the ground, however you may need more strands depending on your deer population's resourcefulness. Electric fencing can be an aesthetically simple way of protecting your garden, but it can also be more expensive, complicated, dangerous for children, and generally ineffective for smaller animals.

Fig. 4
Tall Picket Fence Will Keep Deer Out

- Some gardeners have successfully deterred deer by using a single clear fishing line around the perimeter of the garden, set up at 30 inches above the ground. The deer can't see the fishing line and when they walk into it, they get spooked and run off. Instead of a single line, some set up multiple strands every six inches above the ground. This is a very inexpensive and simple method, however its efficacy is unclear.

Fig. 5 Electric Fence

Rodent-Proof Fencing: The two facets of a successful rodent-proof fence are how to keep the critters from climbing over the fence, and how to keep them from burrowing under. While fencing can be very effective, some rodents, especially gophers and ground squirrels, might still find their way above, below, or through a fence if they are motivated.

Most rodents are good climbers, so the best technique to keep them from climbing over a fence is to leave the top of the fence unsecured to any fence post. This makes the top part of the fence wobbly and unstable for climbing and keeps out all but the most determined rodents.

To keep them from burrowing under the fence, bury the fence vertically below ground. Another option which is frequently just as effective and requires less deep digging is to create an apron. A fence apron is where you bury the fence vertically at first, but then curve the fence horizontally to create an 'L' shape underground that the animals hit whenever they try to burrow.

Regardless of the type of rodent, the fence design is the same while the specific fence dimensions vary (table 1).

Digging to the depths mentioned on Table 1 can be challenging especially in rocky soils. One option is either not to bury the fence at all, or only bury it a few inches and hope that is enough. In some areas, rodents may not be overly interested in your garden.

Fig. 6
If the top of the fence is secured, most rodents can climb over

And if you find a shallow fence is not sufficient, you can always add a deeper fence extension, although it will be more difficult to dig to those depths when the above ground fence is already in place.

Determined rodents are able to chew through plastic and some metal fencing. When choosing a fence material make sure it is at least 16-gauge metal, and any below ground portions of the fence are galvanized or vinyl coated to avoid rusting.

Table 1
Rodent-Proof Fence Dimensions

	Fence Height (including loose top)	Loose Top Height	Vertical Depth (if no apron)	Apron Vertical Depth	Apron Horizontal Length
Mouse	12 inches	6 inches	12 inches	0-3 inches	12 inches
Groundhog	48 inches	18 inches	36 inches	12 inches	24 inches
Ground Squirrel	48 inches	18 inches	24 inches	12 inches	24 inches
Gopher*	12 inches	n/a	36 inches	n/a	n/a
Raccoon	48 inches	18 inches	24 inches	0-3 inches	24 inches

*Gophers do not like to climb, but are incredibly skilled burrowers. Perimeter fencing has only limited effectiveness for gophers. And while a 36 inch fence depth will frequently work, gophers have been known to burrow down 5 feet, which is an unrealistic depth for garden fencing.

Rabbit-Proof Fencing: While rabbits can be extremely destructive to a garden, they are generally the easiest to fence out. They do not climb, so the fence only needs to be two feet high. And while they can burrow, it is nowhere close to the extent of rodents. A below ground fence only needs to be 6-inches deep with a 6 to 8 inch apron.

Fig. 7 Ground Squirrel

Rabbits, like rodents, can gnaw through fencing, therefore make sure it is at least 16-gauge metal and any below ground portions are galvanized or vinyl coated to avoid rusting.

Sidebar 1 Bears

Bears have the potential to wreak havoc on a garden. Making a garden truly 100% bear proof is a mighty large task. Most fences will not stop a determined bear, and while electric fencing can work well, the voltage will need to be much higher than what other wildlife require.

The good news is that unless your bear population is starving, they will normally leave your garden alone. And while a traditional deer/rodent/rabbit fence may not stop a bear, it will lightly deter them. If a bear is merely exploring an area and not determined to access your garden, any type of physical barrier may be enough to stop them.

As well, don't leave rotting organic matter around the garden. While a bear may feel neutral about your kale plant, it will certainly be interested in your smelly compost.

Deer/Rodent/Rabbit–Proof Fencing: It's likely that you may need to protect your garden from not one, but all the major intruders. If that is the case consider combining the characteristics of a good deer fence, rabbit fence and rodent fence. While there are many ways to accomplish this, here is one option:

Construct an eight-foot-tall fence with inexpensive and lightweight mesh netting. Leave the top 18 inches unsecured to the corner posts to deter climbing animals. Then overlap the bottom two feet of the fence with heavier duty 16-gauge galvanized metal fencing to keep rabbits and rodents out. If needed, bury that same 16-gauge galvanized metal fencing either 24 to 36 inches deep or 12 inches deep and with a 24 inch apron.

Row Cover (for deer, rodents, rabbits and birds)

While row cover may not be sturdy enough to truly stop most eager animals, that is not what makes it a great animal deterrent. Instead, its effectiveness lies in its ability to hide and

Fig. 8 Row Cover Hides Plants from Animals

disguise your plants. Most animals that target a garden have poor eyesight (with the exception of birds), and if they don't know there's a tasty plant in front of them, they won't pursue it. And while many of these animals have an excellent sense of smell, most non-flowering garden veggies are not overly aromatic and won't attract animals.

It's important to set up your row cover early before they discover your plants. For most animals, once they find a garden bed it is too late to hide it from them.

However, with birds, unlike with other animals, row cover is not just a disguise, but can work well as a physical barrier. While mammals can easily burrow under or push row cover aside, most birds won't be able to find their way through the row cover to the plants. This makes row cover one of the best options for deterring birds in your garden.

Netting (for birds)

Used in a similar way as row cover, you can cover your plants with a light bird netting. This netting lets air, water, sunlight, and beneficial insects through, but stops birds. It is most effective when it is draped over metal or PVC hoops rather than directly over the plants, since birds may still be able to peck at the plants if the netting isn't raised.

Fig. 9 Bird Netting Over an Entire Garden

Ultrasonic Pest Deterrents (for deer, rodents, and rabbits)

Ultrasonic pest deterrents are small devices that emit an ultrasonic or barely audible noise that mammals don't like. These devices however are not effective against birds, since birds do not have the ability to hear high-pitched ultrasonic noise.

Many of these devices have different settings for different mammals, depending on what you're trying to deter. This noise is not painful to animals, but is annoying. These devices may not be immediately effective, but over the course of a couple of weeks the animals will learn that it's not worth it to visit your garden.

A lot of these devices claim the noise is inaudible to humans, but depending on the setting you choose, some people can hear it. While this noise can be a bit bothersome, so is having all your vegetables eaten.

The best types of ultrasonic pest deterrent are solar powered and motion activated. Whatever type you buy, be sure to check their distance of effectiveness. You may need more than one.

Sprays (for deer, rodents and rabbits)

Spraying your plants, whether with a homemade or commercial spray, is an effective way to keep deer, rodents and rabbits away. These sprays work by covering the intended plants with a very pungent smell and taste. Sometimes an animal will still take a nibble or two but should quickly decide the plants are too

Sidebar 2
Homemade Spray Recipe

Ingredients:

- 5-10 Hot Peppers (or cayenne powder)
- 1 Tbsp. Liquid Soap (not detergent)
- 1-2 Tbsp. Vegetable Oil
- *Optional: 1 Head of Garlic, chopped fine
- 1 Gallon Water

Directions:

1. Combine ingredients
2. Let mixture sit for 24 hours
3. Strain and use

unpalatable to eat.

Unfortunately, the odor from these sprays may leave your garden smelling a bit unpleasant. As well, you will need to carefully wash your harvested veggies to ensure the spray's flavor doesn't affect your food. You also need to re-apply the spray frequently, many times every week and after any rain. Since you can't spray the roots of the plant, these sprays are the least effective for root crops. If you use a commercial spray make sure it is organic and safe for vegetable gardens. It is also fun to make your own spray (see sidebar 2).

Wire Mesh Bed Lining (for rodents)

When constructing your raised beds, you can put a layer of 1/2 inch metal hardware cloth at the base of the bed before filling it with soil. With this lining in place, roots and water will still be able to pass through, however burrowing animals will not.

When installing this lining make sure there is enough space above the lining for the harvestable parts of your root crops to grow. For example, if you plan to grow a carrot in a *Fig. 10 Scarecrow*

lined bed, make sure the carrot can comfortably grow to a depth of 8-12 inches before hitting the mesh lining. Certain crops, like potatoes, require up to 24 inches of space above the lining and therefore may not be appropriate to grow in this type of bed.

This lining will not protect the above ground parts of the plant from animals.

Scaring Away (for birds)

Putting objects in your garden to scare birds away can be an effective technique. These objects include scarecrows, plastic owls, and plastic snakes. While these scare tactics work, birds are relatively smart and unless you frequently move them to different spots in the garden, the birds will realize that the objects never move and are not a threat.

Live Trapping (for rodents and rabbits)

While it is more effective and healthier for the wild ecosystem to use passive deterrents, like fencing, row cover, and sprays, using a more active deterrent like trapping may occasionally make the most sense.

Table 2
Animal
Relocation
Minimum
Distance

Most animals that invade your garden do not act alone and trying to catch every rabbit or squirrel in your area is an unrealistic goal. However, at times, you may be dealing with an individual animal. The most common example of this is with gophers. Gophers are solitary animals, and if you have gopher damage in your garden, it is probably from a single animal.

	Distance
Gopher	5-10 miles
Squirrel	3-5 miles
Mouse	3 miles
Groundhog	5 miles
Rabbit	5 miles

If you choose to trap an animal, use live traps - they are more humane for the animal and healthier for the ecosystem. Just make sure you release the animal far enough away that it can't find its way back to your garden (table 2). Before trapping any animal make sure it is legal to do so in your area.

Crop Choice (for deer, rodents and rabbits)

Fig. 11 Rodent Snacking in a Garden

Trying to figure out what an animal will or won't eat is challenging. The tastes of an individual animal can be as unique as a human's. The crop that was completely spared one year may become their favorite the next. Learning what you can safely grow in your garden will require trial and error. Relying on animal-resistant vegetables is not as effective as some of the other options in this chapter, but they still may help when nothing else works (table 3).

You may notice some similarities between the lists on Table 3. If you have pressure from deer, rodents, and rabbits, you'll have the best luck growing asparagus, alliums (onions, leeks, garlic), and perennial herbs. After that you may try dabbling in the cucurbit family (cucumbers, melons and squash) and the nightshade family (tomatoes, peppers,

Fig. 12 Deer

eggplant, and potatoes). The one crop family that is not on any of these lists are brassicas (kale, cabbage, broccoli etc.). Plants in the brassica family are some of the most prone to being eaten by animals and should be avoided if animals can't be kept out of the garden.

Folk Methods

There are a number of folk remedies for deterring animals. These methods are generally not backed by science, and their results are questionable. Sometimes folk remedies are legitimate and effective techniques that have yet to be validated by western science, and other times they are completely useless. I encourage some skepticism before trying any of these methods.

- Hang bars of soap around the garden
- Sprinkle human hair around the garden
- Place fabric softener sheets around the garden
- Sprinkle dried blood meal around the garden

Using Multiple Methods

None of the methods mentioned in this chapter are 100% effective. A motivated animal is able to overcome any

Deer Resistant	Rodent Resistant	Rabbit Resistant
Asparagus	Asparagus	Asparagus
Allium Family	Allium Family	Allium Family
Perennial Herbs	Perennial Herbs	Perennial Herbs
Eggplant	Tomato*	Tomato
Tomato*	Pepper*	Potato
Potato*	Eggplant*	
Pepper*		
Cucurbit Family*		
Basil*		
Carrots*		
Corn*		
*Moderately prone to damage		

Table 3 Animal Resistant Vegetables

single defense you use. Depending on how determined your wildlife is, the best defense may be to use more than one of the above methods. This may mean having a fence, using row cover, and still needing to live trap the occasional gopher. Or this could mean not having a fence but using a wire mesh net below your raised beds, using a hot pepper spray as well as ultrasonic deterrents. Experiment with the various methods to find what works for you and your garden.

Fig. 13
Rabbit

Pests and Diseases 10

Whether a pest (insect) or a disease (bacteria, virus, or fungus), both function as organisms with a parasitic relationship to plants. These parasitic organisms can stunt plant growth, diminish yields, and ultimately kill their hosts. The good news is that while pests and diseases can be very destructive, there are effective tools to keep your garden healthy. As well, while there are many pests and diseases that can potentially attack your plants, you may go years without encountering any. And in the end, it is unlikely any more than a few will ever find their way into your isolated garden.

Since there are so many potential invaders, and yet so few that you'll actually encounter, you don't have to preemptively deter any individual pest or disease that has not visited your garden. Instead, start with the broad techniques discussed below and only delve into the individual remedies for specific pests and diseases if they become a problem.

Preemptive Care Before Any Pest or Disease is Present

Inspect Your Plants

The number one way to prevent a devastating pest or disease outbreak in your garden is to notice a problem before it gets bad. Dealing with a few aphids or caterpillars is so much easier than dealing with a garden covered in them. Take your time and really inspect your plants. Get close and look for chewed holes in leaves, stunted growth, malformed portions of the plant, or discoloration of the leaves. These are all common signs of a pest or disease. If you do find signs of a pest or disease, use Table 2 to narrow down the possible culprits and then develop a plan to deal with it.

Keep Your Garden Weed-Free

Many times, native plants (aka weeds) are the natural habitat for pests and diseases. By removing weeds from your garden, it is less likely any pests or diseases will spread from a weed to a garden plant.

As well, diseases tend to prefer damp areas with poor air circulation. By removing weeds, you ensure there is adequate air flow between plants.

Fig. 1 Colorado Potato Beetles Eating Potato Leaves

Preemptive Care the Following Year After a Pest or Disease Was in Your Garden

If a specific pest or disease was present one year, you should be on high alert for it coming back again. This means employing the above preemptive care strategies (inspecting your plants and weeding your garden) as well as a few extra techniques.

Grow Resistant Varieties

Many plant varieties have been bred to be resistant to certain pests and diseases. Generally, this does not mean those resistant plants can't become a host for that pest or disease, but it is less likely, and if they do become infected, they will be less affected. While originally pest and disease resistance may not have been your number one priority when choosing plant varieties, it should become a priority once a certain pest or disease is already present in your garden.

Crop Rotation

Crop rotation is discussed in more detail on page 32, but the basic idea is to avoid planting the same crop in the same place in your garden multiple years in a row. If you don't have any pests or diseases in your garden, crop rotation is not a necessity, however if there is an outbreak, crop rotation becomes an important step in returning your garden to a healthy state.

Most pests and diseases only attack certain plants. For example, if there was a Colorado potato beetle infestation in the

Fig. 2
Aphids on the Stem of a Plant

previous year's potato crop, you wouldn't want to plant potatoes (or other members of the nightshade family) in the same place. However, you can plant almost anything else in that infected area and any beetles that overwintered won't hurt those new plants.

If you have an area of your garden that is likely to have a recurrence of a certain pest or disease, use Table 2 to determine what plants are the least susceptible to that specific pest or disease and can be planted in that area. In general, you'll want to rotate your crops based on their plant family. While a pest or disease may have a preferred host plant, most will still attack other members of their preferred host plant's family.

Table 1 Plant Families

Crop Family	Plants
Solanaceae (Nightshade Family)	Eggplants, Peppers, Potatoes, Tomatoes
Brassicaceae (Brassica Family)	Bok Choi, Broccoli, Brussels Sprouts, Cabbage, Cauliflower, Kale, Kohlrabi, Mustard/Asian Greens, Napa Cabbage, Radish, Rutabaga, Turnips
Cucurbitaceae (Cucurbit Family)	Cucumbers, Melons, Summer Squash/Zucchini, Winter Squash
Fabaceae (Legume Family)	Beans, Peas
Amaryllidaceae (Allium Family)	Garlic, Leeks, Onions
Chenopodiaceae (Goosefoot Family)	Beets, Spinach, Swiss Chard
Umbelliferae (Umbel Family)	Carrots, Cilantro, Dill, Parsley, Parsnips
Other	Basil (Mint Family), Corn (Gramineae/Grass Family), Lettuce (Aster Family), Sweet Potatoes (Convolvulaceae/ Morning Glory Family), Asparagus (Asparagaceae Family)

Row Cover

Row cover is a great way of physically blocking certain crops from being attacked by a pest or disease. For example, if you know your garden has flea beetles, you'll want to cover any young brassica family crops, at least until the plants are larger and less susceptible to their damage.

Row cover is also a great tool when used in conjunction with crop rotation. Since most pests can fly or walk, and many diseases travel on those pests, or by wind, row cover can help improve the effectiveness of crop rotation in a small garden.

Row cover only works if you cover the plants before a pest or disease is present. If a pest or disease is already living on a plant, use a different method to eradicate them, and try to cover earlier in the season next year.

Plant with Wider Spacing

Generally, space in a garden is in high demand, and you may want to squeeze in as many plants as possible. Under normal conditions this is a good idea, as long as you still provide the minimum amount of space a plant needs to grow. However, if you expect a disease to make a resurgence in your garden, it may be wise to plant any susceptible plants at a wider than normal spacing to allow for more air circulation between them. By allowing air circulation you keep the plant and the soil drier which makes it harder for a disease to spread.

Fig. 3 Flea Beetle Damage on a Young Brassica

First Signs of a Pest or Disease

At the first signs of a pest or disease, refer to Table 2 to determine what is attacking your plants. Once you know what pest or disease is present in your garden, you can determine which of the below treatment options will be most effective.

Limit Contact with Unhealthy Plants Especially When Wet

If you touch an unhealthy plant, you might pick up spores or small insects that can be passed onto the next plant you touch. This is especially true when touching wet plants. If you must touch an unhealthy plant, do so at the end of your visit to the garden, or at least wash your hands in between contact with unhealthy and healthy plants.

Fig. 4 Diseased Tomato Plant

Hand Pick Insects

Some pests are large enough that the easiest method to control their population is to simply hand pull them off your plants. With this method you may not completely eradicate them, but with enough care and frequent visits you should be able to keep their population small enough that they won't do much damage.

Sprays and Powders

There are a variety of effective and safe organic sprays and powders to use. If you are only spraying a couple of small plants, a household spray bottle will work fine, however if you plan to spray a large area you may want to invest in a larger garden sprayer that you can find at any plant nursery.

Sidebar 1
Soap Spray Recipe

Ingredients:

- 5 Tbsp Liquid Castile Soap
- 1 Gallon Water
- (Optional) 2 Tbsp. Cooking Oil, to help the spray stick to the plant

Directions:

1. Mix Ingredients
2. Spray Directly on Pests

Soap-Based Sprays: These are a great option for killing soft-bodied pests like aphids. However, these sprays only work when directly sprayed onto the pest. Once the spray dries it becomes inert and so should be resprayed frequently, typically every 3-7 days. Test the spray on a couple of leaves and wait 48 hours before spraying the whole plant to make sure the spray won't damage the plant. You can buy these sprays at a nursery or make your own (sidebar 1).

Fig. 5
Tomato
Hornworm

Neem Spray: This are one of the most universally effective natural sprays. It works on a large variety of pests as well as many diseases. You can buy concentrated neem at most nurseries. Plan to spray every 14 days, or every 7 days if the pest or disease problem is severe. Test the spray on a couple of leaves and wait 48 hours before spraying the whole plant to make sure the spray won't damage the plant.

Diatomaceous Earth: This is the ground up fossilized remains of small aquatic animals called diatoms. They are non-toxic to humans and other mammals but deadly to soft bodied insects. The best way to apply diatomaceous earth is either to sprinkle the powder on plants or create a two-inch barrier of it around a garden bed or individual plant. It works best when dry, therefore you will likely need to reapply after rain or irrigation.

Fig. 6
Snail

BT (Bacillus thuringiensis): This is a naturally occurring beneficial bacteria you can spray on your plants that kills a wide variety of pests. This is a safe and organically approved spray. It is most effective when pests are still young, but it works at all stages of development. There are multiple types of BT, so be sure to get the right one for the pest you're targeting.

Pyrethrin: This is an organic pesticide derived from the chrysanthemum plant. While it is organic, it is still a powerful poison. It kills most insects it comes into contact with, including beneficial ones like bees and ladybugs. It does break down rapidly, so it will not build up in the soil, and there is not a high risk of killing beneficial insects beyond the day it is applied.

There are times when pyrethrin may be the best option but be cautious and selective with its use. Test the spray on a couple of leaves and wait 48 hours before spraying the whole plant to make sure the spray won't damage the plant.

Advanced Stage Pest or Disease Problem

If you find yourself with a pest or disease problem that you cannot successfully manage by the above methods, you may need to take more drastic steps.

Beneficial Insects

You can purchase and introduce beneficial insects into your garden to eat specific pests. Beneficial insects have the potential to be extremely effective at controlling a pest *Fig. 7* population without harming the plants. The biggest challenge *Ladybugs* with beneficial insects in an outdoor garden is that they will fly *Eating Aphids*

away once their food source is no longer abundant. That means that they may leave your garden before they have completely eradicated the pest. This can be okay if there isn't enough time left in the season for the pest population to bounce back, or if you are prepared to re-introduce the beneficial insects later in the season.

One method for stopping the beneficial insects from flying away is to cover the infested part of the garden with row cover after you've introduced the insects.

Fig. 8
Late Blight on a Tomato

If you choose to also use an insecticidal spray be sure that it is not harmful to the beneficial insect, or if it is harmful, make sure that it has fully dissipated before introducing them.

You can find live ladybugs for sale at most nurseries, however for other types of beneficial insects you may need to go online to purchase them.

Beneficial Nematodes

Beneficial nematodes are microscopic roundworms that attack certain pest populations but do not harm the host plant. They are only helpful in controlling pests in the soil and do not help control above-ground pests.

There are many different types of beneficial nematodes that all attack different pests. Before purchasing you should know what pest you need to eradicate (see table 2).

Remove Plants

If none of the above methods work, you may need to cut your losses and remove an unhealthy plant. This may feel like a defeat, but it is not. Your goal is to have a healthy and productive garden. Sometimes you may have to remove a plant for the greater good. By physically removing an unhealthy plant, you won't give the pests or diseases living on that plant the opportunity to overwinter in the garden and hurt the next year's crop. And, if you remove the infested or diseased plant with enough time left in the season, you may even be able to plant a different crop in its space which will ultimately be more productive than leaving a dying plant in the ground in the hope of getting a meager harvest before the plant finally dies.

When removing a plant, put all the plant material, including the roots, in the trash rather than composting it or turning it into the soil. Otherwise, the pest or disease may survive the winter and infect the following year's plants.

Sidebar 2
Pests Carry Diseases

One of the most frequent ways a plant disease is introduced into your garden is through a garden pest. By protecting your garden from pests you are also protecting it from various diseases as well.

Pest and Disease Identification

Use the table on the following pages to help identify what specific pest or disease is affecting your plants. Be aware that this table is not comprehensive and only lists the most common garden pests and diseases. As well, soil deficiency can present symptoms similar to many pests and diseases. Refer to chapter 7 (page 66) to learn more about your soil.

The information in this table is grouped by crop family (see table 1) since most pests and diseases attack all members of the same crop family.

Table 2
Pest and Disease Identification and Treatment

	Symptoms	Physical Description of Pest at Time of Damage	Pest or Disease Name	Treatment
Allium Family (Amaryllidaceae) **Garlic, Leeks, Onions**	Gray colored leaves with brown tips	1mm; can fly	Onion thrips	Beneficial insects (minute pirate, lacewing, ladybugs); neem; soap spray; pyrethrins; diatomaceous earth
	Limp wilted plants with yellow leaves	5mm; white or brown larvae	Onion maggots	No treatment although many times plants can still be harvested; crop rotation and row cover should be effective the following year
	Dark mold on bulb	n/a	Smudge	Remove infected plants; grow resistant varieties, rotate crops and improve soil drainage the following year
	Yellow leaf tips; bulb rots	n/a	White rot	Remove infected plants; rotate crops and improve soil drainage the following year
Asparagus (Asparagaceae Family)	Brown scars on the spears	2-4mm; black fly	Asparagus miners	Remove infested plant material including old stalks in the fall
	Disfigured spears with brown marks	8mm; orange/red with black dots	Asparagus beetles	Hand pick; spray pyrethrins; remove old dead plant material in the fall
	Leaves eaten off the mature fronds	4-35mm; green larvae	Beet armyworms	BT; neem; beneficial insects (trichogramma wasps, lacewing, ladybugs)
	Young spears eaten or nibbled	5-20mm; brown larvae, typically only visible at night	Cutworms	Beneficial nematodes; trichogramma wasps; diatomaceous earth
	Fronds turning gray	1mm; can fly	Onion thrips	Beneficial insects (minute pirate, lacewing, ladybugs); neem; soap spray; pyrethrins; diatomaceous earth

Table 2
Pest and Disease Identification and Treatment (continued)

	Symptoms	Physical Description of Pest at Time of Damage	Pest or Disease Name	Treatment
Asparagus (continued)	Holes in leaves, with silvery slime trail	5 or more mm; brown; with or without a shell	Slugs or snails	Hand pick; soap spray; neem; diatomaceous earth
	Stunted growth	1-3mm; varied colors; they tend to cluster in groups	Aphids	Hand pick; soap spray; neem; beneficial insects (ladybugs, lacewing, hoverfly), diatomaceous earth
	Red powdery blisters	n/a	Rust	Neem; remove infected leaves
	Small, limp spears with lesions around soil level	n/a	Fusarium wilt	Remove plant, including roots; grow resistant varieties
Brassica Family (Brassicaceae) **Bok Choi, Broccoli, Brussels Sprouts, Cabbage, Cauliflower, Kale, Kohlrabi, Mustard/Asian Greens, Napa Cabbage, Radish, Rutabaga, Turnips**	Stunted growth; wilted and malformed leaves	1-3mm; varied colors; they tend to cluster in groups	Aphids	Hand pick; soap spray; neem; beneficial insects (ladybugs, lacewing, hoverfly), diatomaceous earth
	Gray streaks through leaves	1mm; can fly	Thrips	Beneficial insects (minute pirate, lacewing, ladybugs); neem; soap spray; pyrethrins; diatomaceous earth
	Large holes in leaves	4-20mm; green larvae	Cabbageworm (cabbage looper)	Hand pick; soap spray; neem; BT, pyrethrin

Table 2
Pest and Disease Identification and Treatment (continued)

	Symptoms	Physical Description of Pest at Time of Damage	Pest or Disease Name	Treatment
Brassicas (continued)	Holes in leaves, with silvery slime trail	5 or more mm; brown; with or without a shell	Slugs or snails	Hand pick; soap spray; neem; diatomaceous earth
	Multiple small holes in leaves	1-2mm; black, quick jumpers	Flea beetles	Pyrethrins; plants only damaged by flea beetles when young- use row cover for the first month
	Limp, wilted plant on sunny days	3-6mm; white or brown maggots	Cabbage maggots	Diatomaceous earth; beneficial nematodes
	Wilted light colored leaves	n/a	Root knot nematodes	Beneficial nematodes (limited success); soaking soil with neem (limited success); grow resistant varieties
	Outer leaves turn brown and die	n/a	Head rot	Remove infected plants; rotate crops
	Slow growth with brown areas on leaves	n/a	Black rot	Remove infected plants; grow resistant varieties; rotate crops
	Slow growth, wilted leaves, swollen roots	n/a	Club root	Remove infected plants; grow resistant varieties; rotate crops
	Dark blemishes on stem and leaves	n/a	Blackleg	Remove infected plants; grow resistant varieties; rotate crops
	Brown spots, and dry leaves	n/a	Alternaria leaf spot	Soap spray; neem; pyrethrins

Table 2
Pest and Disease Identification and Treatment (continued)

	Symptoms	Physical Description of Pest at Time of Damage	Pest or Disease Name	Treatment
Brassicas (continued)	Spotty yellow on top of leaves, white mold on underside of leaves	n/a	Downy mildew	Neem; use drip irrigation or carefully hand water to avoid getting leaves wet
	White powder on leaves	n/a	Powdery mildew	Neem; remove diseased foliage; prune to allow more air circulation
	Stunted growth, yellow leaves	n/a	Yellows	Remove infected plants; rotate crop and use row cover the following year
	Fuzzy gray mold on leaves	n/a	Botrytis	Prune infected plant material
Cucurbit Family (Cucurbitaceae) **Cucumbers, Melons, Summer Squash/ Zucchini, Winter Squash**	Holes in leaves	5mm; yellow and black striped or spotted beetle	Cucumber beetle	Hand pick; beneficial insects (ladybugs. lacewing, spined soldier bugs); pyrethrins
	Wilted vines	14mm; brown larvae	Squash vine borers	Pyrethrins
	Yellow leaves with sticky residue	1mm: white	Whiteflies	Soap spray; neem; pyrethrins; beneficial insects (ladybugs, lacewings)
	Small yellow dots on leaves	1mm; light colored	Spider mites	Soap spray; pyrethrin; neem; beneficial insects (ladybugs, lacewing. minute pirate bug, predatory mites)

Table 2
Pest and Disease Identification and Treatment (continued)

	Symptoms	Physical Description of Pest at Time of Damage	Pest or Disease Name	Treatment
Cucurbits (continued)	Light colored spots on leaves; new growth is wilted and black	8-14mm; brown	Squash bugs	Hand pick; diatomaceous earth; neem; pyrethrins
	Malformed leaves and shoots	1-3mm; varied colors; they tend to cluster in groups	Aphids	Hand pick; soap spray; neem; beneficial insects (ladybugs, lacewing, hoverfly), diatomaceous earth
	Angular yellow or dead spots on leaves	n/a	Angular leaf spot	Soap spray; neem; pyrethrins
	Plant wilts after waterings	n/a	Bacterial wilt	Row cover uninfected plants; no treatment for infected plants
	Yellow spots on top of leaves with gray mold on underside of leaves	n/a	Downy Mildew	Neem; use drip irrigation or carefully hand water to avoid getting leaves wet
	White powder on leaves	n/a	Powdery Mildew	Neem; remove diseased foliage; prune to allow more air circulation
	Brown dead spots on leaves; indented dead spots on fruit	n/a	Anthracnose	Neem; remove infected leaves
	Small or malformed leaves	n/a	Mosaic	Remove infected plant material or entire plant; rotate crop and use row cover the following year

Table 2
Pest and Disease Identification and Treatment (continued)

	Symptoms	Physical Description of Pest at Time of Damage	Pest or Disease Name	Treatment
Cucurbits (continued)	Leaves and branches wilt and die; fruit rots	n/a	Fusarium rot	Remove plant, including roots; grow resistant varieties
	Blossoms wilt and die; the fruit rots from the stem side (only affects squash)	n/a	Choanephora wet-rot	Remove infected plants; grow resistant varieties; rotate crops
	Spots on the fruit	n/a	Black rot	Remove infected plants; grow resistant varieties; rotate crops
	Fuzzy gray mold on leaves	n/a	Botrytis	Prune infected plant material
Goosefoot Family (Chenopodiaceae) Beets, Spinach, Swiss Chard	Translucent, white or brown sections of leaves, possibly in lines	2mm; white/gray larvae	Leafminers	Soap spray; neem; parasitic wasps
	Holes eaten through on leaves	4-35mm; green larvae	Beet armyworms	BT; neem; beneficial insects (trichogramma wasps, lacewing, ladybugs)
	Wilted, malformed leaves	1-3mm; varied colors; they tend to cluster in groups	Aphids	Hand pick; soap spray; neem; beneficial insects (ladybugs, lacewing, hoverfly), diatomaceous earth
	Large holes in leaves	Varied size; green or yellow	Caterpillars	Hand pick; soap spray; neem; BT, pyrethrin

Table 2
Pest and Disease Identification and Treatment (continued)

	Symptoms	Physical Description of Pest at Time of Damage	Pest or Disease Name	Treatment
Goosefoots (continued)	Multiple small holes in leaves	1-2mm; black, quick jumpers	Flea beetles	Pyrethrins; plants only damaged by flea beetles when young- use row cover for the first month
	Holes in leaves, with silvery slime trail	5 or more mm; brown; with or without a shell	Slugs or snails	Hand pick; soap spray; neem; diatomaceous earth
	White or gray mold on underside of leaf	n/a	Downy mildew	Neem; use drip irrigation or carefully hand water to avoid getting leaves wet
	Small dark or yellow spots on leaves	n/a	Rust	Neem; remove infected leaves
	Fuzzy gray mold on leaves	n/a	Botrytis	Prune infected plant material
	Wilting, yellowing leaves	n/a	Fusarium wilt	Remove plant, including roots; grow resistant varieties
Legume Family (Fabaceae) Beans, Peas	Small bumps on pods	4-12mm; brown; angular body; 6 legs; large antenna	Stink bugs	Hand pick; soap spray; neem; diatomaceous earth
	Small holes in seeds	3-5mm; brown; round body; 6 legs; large antenna	Weevils	Diatomaceous earth; beneficial nematodes
	Misshapen young leaves that turn yellow	4-6mm; brown with yellow/green lines	Tarnished Plant Bugs	Soap spray; pyrethrin; neem
	Withered yellow leaves	1-3mm; varied colors; they tend to cluster in groups	Aphids	Hand pick; soap spray; neem; beneficial insects (ladybugs, lacewing, hoverfly), diatomaceous earth

Table 2
Pest and Disease Identification and Treatment (continued)

	Symptoms	Physical Description of Pest at Time of Damage	Pest or Disease Name	Treatment
Legumes (continued)	Holes in leaves, with silvery slime trail	5 or more mm; brown; with or without a shell	Slugs or snails	Hand pick; soap spray; neem; diatomaceous earth
	Light speckles on leaves	1mm; light colored	Spider mites	Soap spray; pyrethrin; neem; beneficial insects (ladybugs, lacewing. minute pirate bug, predatory mites)
	Translucent leaves	6mm; orange with black dots	Mexican bean beetle	Hand pick; neem; pyrethrin
	Large holes in leaves	5mm; black/yellow	Bean leaf beetles	Hand pick
	Large holes in leaves	Varied size; green or yellow	Caterpillars	Hand pick; soap spray; neem; BT, pyrethrin
	Scar damage on pods	1mm; can fly	Thrips	Beneficial insects (minute pirate, lacewing, ladybugs); neem; soap spray; pyrethrins; diatomaceous earth
	Holes in individual peas	3-5mm; white or green larvae	Pea moths	Pyrethrins if infestation is sever; generally you can still get get good harvests when moths are present
	Winding translucent lines through leaves	2mm; white/gray larvae	Pea leafminers	Soap spray; neem; parasitic wasps
	Water filled spots, red colored leaves	n/a	Halo blight	Remove infected plants; grow resistant varieties; rotate crops
	Dark colored warts on underside of leaves and pods	n/a	Rust	Neem; remove infected leaves

Table 2
Pest and Disease Identification and Treatment (continued)

	Symptoms	Physical Description of Pest at Time of Damage	Pest or Disease Name	Treatment
Legumes (continued)	Fuzzy gray mold on leaves and pods	n/a	Botrytis	Prune infected plant material
	Dark colored lines on leaves with spots on pods	n/a	Anthracnose	Neem; remove infected leaves
	Oddly shaped leaves with rough spots on pods	n/a	Mosaic	Remove infected plant material or entire plant; rotate crop and use row cover the following year
	Stunted growth, yellowing lower leaves	n/a	Fusarium wilt	Remove plant, including roots; grow resistant varieties
	Dark spots on leaves, stem and/or pods	n/a	Blight	Remove infected plants; grow resistant varieties and rotate crops the following year
	White powder on leaves	n/a	Powdery mildew	Neem; remove diseased foliage; prune to allow more air circulation
Lettuce (Asteraceae Family)	Misshapen or curled leaves	1-3mm; varied colors; they tend to cluster in groups	Aphids	Hand pick; soap spray; neem; beneficial insects (ladybugs, lacewing, hoverfly), diatomaceous earth
	Gray lines on leaves	1mm; can fly	Thrips	Beneficial insects (minute pirate, lacewing, ladybugs); neem; soap spray; pyrethrins; diatomaceous earth
	Holes in leaves, with silvery slime trail	5 or more mm; brown; with or without a shell	Slugs or snails	Hand pick; soap spray; neem; diatomaceous earth

Table 2
Pest and Disease Identification and Treatment (continued)

	Symptoms	Physical Description of Pest at Time of Damage	Pest or Disease Name	Treatment
Lettuce (continued)	Stunted growth	n/a	Root knot nematodes	Beneficial nematodes (limited success); soaking soil with neem (limited success); grow resistant varieties
	Dark colored rot starting at the bottom of plant	n/a	Rhizoctonia bottom rot	Remove infected plants; grow resistant varieties, use crop rotation and improve soil drainage for the following year
	Leaf veins turned yellow	n/a	Big vein	Ignore light damage; remove plant if severe; grow resistant varieties the following year; crop rotation won't help
	Rot starting at the bottom of plant	n/a	Sclerotinia drop	Remove infected plants; grow resistant varieties, use crop rotation and improve soil drainage for the following year
	Stunted growth, yellowing leaves	n/a	Corky root	Remove infected plants including their roots; grow resistant varieties, use crop rotation following year
	Light colored spots on leaves; white mold on underside of leaf	n/a	Downy mildew	Neem; use drip irrigation or carefully hand water to avoid getting leaves wet
	White powder on leaves	n/a	Powdery mildew	Neem; remove diseased foliage; prune to allow more air circulation
	Fuzzy gray mold on leaves	n/a	Botrytis	Prune and throw out infected plant material
	Stunted and malformed young leaves	n/a	Aster yellows	Remove infected plants; rotate crop and use row cover the following year

Table 2
Pest and Disease Identification and Treatment (continued)

	Symptoms	Physical Description of Pest at Time of Damage	Pest or Disease Name	Treatment
Lettuce (continued)	Stunted, malformed and yellowing young leaves	n/a	Mosaic	Remove infected plant material or entire plant; rotate crop and use row cover the following year
Nightshade Family (Solanaceae) **Eggplant, Peppers, Potatoes, Tomatoes**	Yellowing dead spots on leaves	2-30mm; varied colors	Leafhoppers	Hand pick; soap spray; diatomaceous earth; beneficial insects for egg and larval stages (ladybugs, lacewing, minute pirate bugs)
	Large holes in leaves	6-11mm; striped yellow and black body with orange head	Colorado potato beetle	Hand pick; BT; pyrethrins; beneficial insects (spined soldier bugs, parasitic wasps)
	Holes in leaves, with silvery slime trail	5 or more mm; brown; with or without a shell	Slugs or snails	Hand pick; soap spray; neem; diatomaceous earth
	Yellowing and malformed flowers and fruit	2-3mm; dark round body	Weevils	Diatomaceous earth; beneficial nematodes
	Stunted growth; wilted and malformed leaves	1-3mm; varied colors; they tend to cluster in groups	Aphids	Hand pick; soap spray; neem; beneficial insects (ladybugs, lacewing, hoverfly), diatomaceous earth
	Winding translucent lines through leaves	1-2mm; yellow/green larvae	Leafminers	Soap spray; neem; parasitic wasps
	Small yellow dots on leaves	1mm; light colored	Spider mites	Soap spray; pyrethrin; neem; beneficial insects (ladybugs, lacewing. minute pirate bug, predatory mites)

Table 2
Pest and Disease Identification and Treatment (continued)

	Symptoms	Physical Description of Pest at Time of Damage	Pest or Disease Name	Treatment
Nightshades (continued)	Multiple small holes in leaves	1-2mm; black, quick jumpers	Flea beetles	Pyrethrins; plants only damaged by flea beetles when young- use row cover for the first month
	New potato growth wilts and dies	3-6mm; cream colored larvae	Potato tuberworm	Remove infected plants; rotate crops and plant deep the following year
	Large holes in leaves	Varied size; green or yellow	Caterpillars	Hand pick; soap spray; neem; BT, pyrethrin
	Small tunnels on and through potato tubers	1-2mm; black	Tuber flea beetles	The following year rotate crops; use row cover; spray pyrethrins; beneficial nematodes
	Holes through tomato fruits	15-35mm; brown or green larvae	Tomato fruitworm	Handpick; BT, beneficial nematodes; pyrethrins; neem
	Entire tomato leaves eaten	25-80mm; green with a horn on its head	Tomato hornworm	Hand pick; diatomaceous earth; beneficial insects for eggs (lacewing, trichogramma wasps, ladybugs)
	Dead spots on leaves and fruit	n/a	Bacterial spot	No treatment; generally not fatal; grow resistant varieties and rotate crops the following year
	Dead spots on leaves	n/a	Leaf spot	Soap spray; neem; pyrethrins
	Stunted growth; and malformed leaves, stems and fruit	n/a	Mosaic	Remove infected plant material or entire plant; rotate crop and use row cover the following year
	Yellowing dead spots on leaves; and/or rotten sections of fruit	n/a	Late blight	Remove infected plants; grow resistant varieties; rotate crops

Table 2
Pest and Disease Identification and Treatment (continued)

	Symptoms	Physical Description of Pest at Time of Damage	Pest or Disease Name	Treatment
Nightshades (continued)	Yellowing dead spots on leaves	n/a	Early blight	Remove infected leaves
	Stunted growth, yellowing lower leaves	n/a	Fusarium wilt	Remove plant, including roots; grow resistant varieties
	Fuzzy gray mold on leaves	n/a	Botrytis	Prune infected plant material
	Stunted growth and yellowing leaves	n/a	Root knot nematodes	Beneficial nematodes (limited success); soaking soil with neem (limited success); grow resistant varieties
	Dark scabs on tubers	n/a	Scab	Rotate crops the following year
	Indented areas on fruit	n/a	Anthracnose	Neem; remove infected leaves
	Dark hard spots on leaves; indented areas on fruit	n/a	Alternaria blight	Remove infected plants; grow resistant varieties; rotate crops
	Dark colored lower leaves on tomatoes	n/a	Tomato russet mites	Soap spray; neem; pyrethrin; beneficial nematodes
	Stunted growth and wilting leaves	n/a	Bacterial wilt	Row cover uninfected plants; no treatment for infected plants
Sweet Corn (Gramineae Family)	Kernals and silks eaten	20-25mm; red or light brown larvae	Corn earworms	BT; beneficial nematodes; pyrethrins; open tip of husk and remove larvae; neem

Table 2
Pest and Disease Identification and Treatment (continued)

	Symptoms	Physical Description of Pest at Time of Damage	Pest or Disease Name	Treatment
Sweet Corn (continued)	Kernals and silks eaten	25mm; gray larvae with brown spots	European corn borers	BT (if on ears or leaves); neem (if on leaves); pyrethrins (if on leaves)
	Silks eaten	5-20mm; brown	Earwigs	Diatomaceous earth
	Slow growth and wilted plants	6mm; yellow and black beetle	Corn rootworms	Beneficial nematodes
	Yellow leaves and plants wilt in the sun	1-3mm; blue/gray	Corn root aphids	Hand pick; soap spray; neem; beneficial insects (ladybugs, lacewing, hoverfly), diatomaceous earth
	Translucent leaves	15mm; black and reddish brown	Japanese beetle	Hand pick; soap spray; neem; beneficial nematodes; BT
	Spots or discoloration on leaves	n/a	Anthracnose	Neem; remove infected leaves
	Spots or discoloration on leaves	n/a	Bacterial leaf spot	Soap spray; neem; pyrethrins
	Slow growth, wilted plants, and yellow streaks on young leaves	n/a	Bacterial wilt	Row cover uninfected plants; no treatment for infected plants
	Round, brown pustules on leaves	n/a	Rust	Neem; remove infected leaves
	Black lumps on ears, leaves and stem	n/a	Corn smut	Hand pick black lumps

Table 2
Pest and Disease Identification and Treatment (continued)

	Symptoms	Physical Description of Pest at Time of Damage	Pest or Disease Name	Treatment
Sweet Potatoes (Convolvulaceae Family)	Multiple small holes in leaves	1-2mm; black, quick jumpers	Sweet potato flea beetles	Pyrethrins; plants only damaged by flea beetles when young- use row cover for the first month
	Holes through roots	5-8mm; white larvae	Sweet potato weevils	Diatomaceous earth; beneficial nematodes
	Yellowing leaves; dark spots on tubers	n/a	Black rot	Remove infected plants; grow resistant varieties; rotate crops
	Stunted growth; small tubers with dark spots	n/a	Pox	Remove infected plants; rotate crops
	Stunted growth and yellowing leaves	n/a	Root knot nematodes	Beneficial nematodes (limited success); soaking soil with neem (limited success); grow resistant varieties
	Yellowing wilted leaves	n/a	Fusarium wilt	Remove plant, including roots; grow resistant varieties
Umbel Family (Umbelliferae) **Carrots, Cilantro, Dill, Parsley, Parsnips**	Holes through roots	8mm; white or yellow larvae	Carrot rust flies	Remove infected plants; rotate crop and use row cover the following year
	Holes through roots	2-4mm; white or yellow larvae	Carrot weevils	Diatomaceous earth; beneficial nematodes
	Holes through roots	6mm; orange worm	Wireworms	Beneficial nematodes; pyrethrins based soil drenches (limited success)

Table 2
Pest and Disease Identification and Treatment (continued)

	Symptoms	Physical Description of Pest at Time of Damage	Pest or Disease Name	Treatment
Umbels (continued)	Wilted light colored leaves	n/a	Root knot nematodes	Beneficial nematodes (limited success); soaking soil with neem (limited success); grow resistant varieties
	Rotting roots	n/a	Black rot	Remove infected plants; grow resistant varieties; rotate crops
	Pale spots on leaves that turn brown and die	n/a	Leaf spot	Soap spray; neem; pyrethrins
	Main root has many thin hairy roots coming off of it	n/a	Aster yellows	Remove infected plants; rotate crop and use row cover the following year

Part Three

Plant Index

Plant Index

This section lists the growing parameters of the most common garden vegetables. Below are a few notes on terminology and how to interpret the information in this section.

Adjusting 'Days to Maturity' for Season Extension Techniques

The planting dates given in this section assume you will not use any season extension techniques. If you use row cover, cloches, weed mat, raised beds, low tunnels, or cold frames, adjust your planting dates accordingly.

- If you use row cover or cloches you can direct seed or transplant outdoors 1-2 weeks earlier in the spring and expect them to survive 1-2 weeks later into the fall.
- If using weed mat you can direct seed or transplant outdoors 1 week earlier in the spring, except for frost sensitive plants that still need to be seeded or transplanted after the risk of frost.
- If using raised beds you can direct seed or transplant outdoors 1 week earlier in the spring, except for frost sensitive plants that still need to be seeded or transplanted after the risk of frost.
- If using low tunnels or cold frames you can direct seed or transplant 3-4 weeks earlier in the spring and expect them to survive 3-4 weeks later into the fall.

While it may be tempting, using multiple season extension techniques at the same time doesn't necessarily mean you can combine their benefits to allow for an even earlier planting date. Just because you use row cover, which allows you to plant 2 weeks earlier, and weed mat, which allows you to plant one week earlier, that doesn't necessarily mean you can add their benefits together and plant 3 weeks earlier. The benefits of using multiple season extension techniques at the same time won't always translate so neatly. There are limits to all these techniques, and with some trial and error you will learn what will and won't work in your garden.

Sunlight

When describing the light requirements of plants, the three terms used are: *full sun, light shade,* and *partial shade. Full sun* means 8 or more hours of direct sunlight each day. *Light shade* means 5-8 hours of direct sunlight each day. And *partial shade* means 2-5 hours of direct sunlight each day. *Full shade* would be less than 2 hours of sunlight and it is not recommended to grow vegetables in those conditions.

Growing Care

The 'Growing Care' section for each plant lists any special steps to take during the growing season. If there is no 'Growing Care' section for a specific plant then they don't require any special care beyond the normal watering, weeding, sidedressing etc.

Plants Want to Survive

In the end, all the information in this section is merely the ideal growing parameters for a specific plant. But remember, plants want to survive even more than you want them to. Even if your garden doesn't have the ideal growing conditions for a certain plant, that doesn't mean that plant won't be able to grow. That plant may not grow as well as it would under ideal conditions, but it may still survive and produce some food.

High Altitude Growing Score

The high altitude growing score is this book's unique rating system that allows you to quickly understand the ease and suitability of growing a plant at high altitudes. It can be a daunting task to synthesize all the facts and numbers in this section to decide what to grow in your garden. And while all that information is important, this rating system is one way of summing it all up into something a bit easier to absorb.

The unique characteristics of all the many different high altitude climates makes creating a universal rating system difficult, so for this rating system it is assuming a cold, short season, windy, dry climate. In general, cold weather crops will get a better score than warm weather crops. As well, plants that you grow for their leaves will get a better score than root crops which will get a better score than fruiting crops. This is because as plants progress through their life cycle, any environmental stressors, such as excessively cold or hot weather, drought, soil deficiencies, critter attacks, or damage from a pest or disease, will have a more pronounced and detrimental effect on their health.

The scoring system is 1-10, with one being the easiest to grow and ten being the hardest.

Asparagus
Asparagaceae Family

Asparagus is one of the few perennial vegetables that is hardy enough to survive at high altitudes. It is a forgiving and easy plant to grow if you have the patience to wait the necessary 2-3 years after planting to begin harvesting. It is cold hardy, drought tolerant, and produces food earlier in the spring than almost anything else in your garden.

High Altitude Growing Score: 2

Length of Season

- *Days to Maturity:* Perennial, harvest the second or third year
- *Frost Tolerant:* Yes
- *Perennial Hardiness:* Zone 3
- *Planting:* Plant living crowns in the spring after the last frost. If your local nursery doesn't sell the crowns, you can order them online.

Soil Conditions

- *Ideal pH:* 6.0-8.0
- *Side Dressing:* 2x/season with an equal N-P-K ratio fertilizer (ex. 5-5-5)
  - *First Year:* Once in the summer and again in the fall
  - *Subsequent Years:* In the spring after the harvest season and again in the fall

Light and Air

- *Light:* Full sun preferred, light shade tolerated
- *Air Temperature (ideal):* 60-70°F

Seed to Seedling

- *Planting Crowns:* Plant crowns 8-12 inches apart in 5-8 inch deep furrows that are 12 inches wide. Cover crowns with 2-3 inches of soil and slowly add more soil as the plants begin to grow above the soil line.
- *Transplant or Direct Seed:* Transplant

Growing Care

- Asparagus is a perennial that will live for many years, but it does not out-compete native weeds very well. Unlike annuals that you can start new every year, with asparagus you need to be especially careful to keep the weeds at bay.
- Fully grown asparagus ferns can get rather large. When choosing a

garden location, keep this in mind so they don't cast shade on other garden crops. Consider growing on the northern edge of the garden.

- By the time a plant is three years old, it will have an extensive root system and will be very drought tolerant, but up until that point regular waterings are needed.

Harvesting

- Harvest when the spears are 6-10 inches tall, and the head of the asparagus is still tight and has not opened. Snap or cut the spears at or below the soil line.
- For the first year after planting it is best not to harvest any of the asparagus, so the plant can use all its energy to establish itself in the soil. Harvest very lightly in the second year and then a normal harvest can begin in the third year. While it may be difficult not to pick asparagus for the first year or two, think of it as an investment in a healthy plant, that once established in your garden, can survive for 25 years.

Storage

- Store in the refrigerator.

Tips

- Hybrids tend to be more productive than heirloom varieties.

Basil

Mint Family

Fresh basil from a garden is a real treat, but due to its preference for warm weather it can be moderately challenging to grow in cold climates. Choose a fast-growing variety and avoid the temptation to plant outside too early.

High Altitude Growing Score: 6

Length of Season

- *Days to Maturity (from transplant):* 30-60 days
- *Frost Tolerant:* No
- *First Direct Seeding or Transplanting:* When soil temperatures reach at least 55°F or 2-4 weeks after the last spring frost.
- *Last Transplanting:* 51-81 days before the first fall frost, depending on the variety's 'Days to Maturity'. Plant earlier to allow for an extended harvest period.
    - *To Calculate Last Planting:* (First fall frost date) minus (days to maturity) minus (21 days to adjust for fall's short days and cold weather)

Soil Conditions

- *Ideal pH:* 5.5-7.0
- *Soil Germination Temperature:* 55-95°F
- *Side Dressing:* Not necessary

Light and Air

- *Light:* Full sun preferred, light shade tolerated
- *Air Temperature (ideal):* 70-90°F

Seed to Seedling

- *Plant Spacing:* 4-8 inch spacing with rows 12-18 inches apart or a uniform 8 inch spacing
- *Seed Depth:* 1/4-1/2 inch
- *Days to Germination:* 7-14 days
- *Transplant or Direct Seed:* Either
- *Days from Germination to Transplanting:* 35-42 days

Growing Care

- The secret to a long season of healthy basil is to never let it flower. If you see flowers beginning to form, cut that stem off above the next growing node. Even if you don't need any basil in that moment you should still cut it back, otherwise the plant will produce flowers and then seeds, and then die.

Harvesting

- Basil can begin being harvested when it is 8-10 inches tall. Pinch or cut off sprigs of basil just below a branching node, as this is where new basil stems will grow from.

Storage

- Once picked, basil does not store well in the refrigerator. The best way to store your basil is to put the sprigs in an open jar on a countertop with an inch of water, making sure that only the stem is submerged in water and not the leaves. The stems will absorb water in the same way a cut flower does in a vase.

Beans

Legume (fabaceae) Family

Beans, like most warm season fruiting vegetables can be challenging to grow at high altitudes. However, due to their relatively quick growth and prolific fruitings, they are easier to grow than most other warm season crops. If you want to venture away from only growing cold hardy crops, beans are a great plant to start with.

High Altitude Growing Score: 6

Length of Season

- *Days to Maturity (from seed):* 48-95 days
- *Frost Tolerant:* No
- *First Direct Seeding or Transplanting:* When soil temperatures reach at least 55°F and it's past the last spring frost.
- *Last Direct Seeding:* 62-109 days before the first fall frost, depending on the variety's 'Days to Maturity'. Plant earlier to allow for an extended harvest period.
    - *To Calculate Last Planting:* (First fall frost date) minus (days to maturity) minus (14 days to adjust for fall's short days and cold weather)

Soil Conditions

- *Ideal pH:* 6.0-7.5
- *Soil Germination Temperature:* 55-85°F
- *Side Dressing:* Not necessary

Light and Air

- *Light:* Full sun
- *Air Temperature (ideal):* 60-70°F

Seed to Seedling

- *Plant Spacing:*
    - *Pole Beans:* 8 inch spacing with rows 12 inches apart, trellis needed
    - *Bush Beans:* 2-4 inch spacing with rows 18-36 inches apart or a uniform 10 inch spacing, no trellis needed
- *Seed Depth:* 1 inch
- *Days to Germination:* 4-10 days
- *Transplant or Direct Seed:* Direct seeding is preferred because their roots are very fragile and do not like to be transplanted, however transplanting is possible if you are very careful
- *Days from Germination to Transplanting:* 21 days

Growing Care

- Pole beans require trellising. Bush beans do not.

Harvesting

- For the best flavor and consistency, pick beans young.
- Pole beans will continue producing for the entire season as long as you consistently harvest the beans before they become overripe. Unpicked beans trigger the plant to end its fruiting stage.

Storage

- Store in the refrigerator.

Tips

- Bean varieties are either indeterminate (pole beans) or determinate (bush beans). When a bean is determinate it produces a large amount of beans in a short period of time and then stops fruiting. With indeterminate growth, the plant continually gives small amounts of beans throughout the season. Generally, determinate bush beans grow faster than indeterminate pole beans.
- If you are trying to fit a later season bean succession in before the first fall frost, consider a determinate bean so you'll get a large flush of beans before the frost rather than an extended harvest from an indeterminate bean that may be cut short by the fall frost.
- Carefully picking an appropriate variety for your climate is always important, but especially when growing warm season crops. Choose wisely.

Beets

Goosefoot (chenopodiaceae) Family

Beets are cold hardy and quick growing. They are an easy and forgiving crop that thrives in the spring and fall, yet still grows well in the summer heat. They are harvestable at any size, so if for whatever reason they do not grow as big as you'd like, they can still be enjoyed small. One challenge is that burrowing animals are prone to eating the roots, and other animals like rabbits and deer may eat the leaves.

High Altitude Growing Score: 2

Length of Season

- *Days to Maturity (from seed):* 50-80 days
- *Frost Tolerant:* Yes
- *First Direct Seeding or Transplanting:* When soil temperatures reach at least 40-50°F <u>or</u> 2-4 weeks before the last spring frost.
- *Last Direct Seeding:* 50-80 days before the first fall frost, depending on the variety's 'Days to Maturity'. Beets will survive for a few weeks after the first fall frost, however they will not produce much new growth due to the cold temperatures and lack of sun.
  - *To Calculate Last Planting:* (First fall frost date) minus (days to maturity)

Soil Conditions

- *Ideal pH:* 6.5-8.0
- *Soil Germination Temperature:* 45-85°F
- *Side Dressing:* 1x/season
  - *Timing:* When plants are 4-5 inches tall
  - *Fertilizer Type:* Equal N-P-K ratio fertilizer (ex. 5-5-5)

Light and Air

- *Light:* Full sun preferred, light shade tolerated
- *Air Temperature (ideal):* 60-75°F

Seed to Seedling

- *Plant Spacing After Thinning:* 3 inch spacing with rows 12-18 inches apart <u>or</u> a uniform 6-8 inch spacing
- *Plant Spacing Before Thinning:* 1-2 seeds/inch with rows 12-18 inches apart <u>or</u> 3-4 seeds every 6-8 inches
- *Seed Depth:* 1/4-1/2 inch
- *Days to Germination:* 5-8 days
- *Transplant or Direct Seed:* Either. Traditionally beets are direct

seeded because they grow so quickly, but transplanting works well if desired.

- *Days from Germination to Transplanting:* 28 days

Growing Care

- Plant spacing and thinning is very important with root crops. If plants are allowed to grow too close together they will not produce large roots.

Harvesting

- Beets can grow very large, and while it may sound appealing to grow a giant beet, their flavor and consistency begins to decline as they get larger than 3 inches in diameter.

Storage

- Store in the refrigerator.
- Cut the leaves from the roots if storing for more than a couple of days. The leaves will continue to draw moisture and nutrients from the root, which will diminish the taste and shelf life of the root.

Tips

- Hybrids beets tend to be sweeter than heirloom varieties and generally produce nicer greens.
- While the leaves and roots of all beet varieties are edible, some varieties have been bred for better root production, others for leaf production, and some for both. Choose the variety that will be the most productive for your needs.

Bok Choi
Brassica (brassicaceae) Family

Bok choi may be a lesser known garden vegetable, but it is an excellent plant for high altitudes. It is fast growing and cold hardy. It can be grown as baby loose-leaf greens, in a similar manner to spinach or mustard greens, or it can be grown as a full head, in a similar manner to napa cabbage.

High Altitude Growing Score: 2

Length of Season

- *Days to Maturity (from seed):* 21-28 (baby) 45-60 (full head)
- *Frost Tolerant:* Yes
- *First Direct Seeding or Transplanting:* When soil temperatures reach at least 45°F <u>or</u> 4 weeks before the last spring frost.
- *Last Direct Seeding:* 21-60 days before the first fall frost, depending on the variety's 'Days to Maturity' and if grown as a full head or loose leaf baby greens.
  - *To Calculate Last Planting:* (First fall frost date) minus (days to maturity) plus (an additional 7 days for growth after first frost)

Soil Conditions

- *Ideal pH:* 6.0-7.5
- *Soil Germination Temperature:* 45-95°F
- *Side Dressing:* 1x/season
  - *Timing:* One month after planting
  - *Fertilizer Type:* High nitrogen fertilizer (ex. 5-0-0)

Light and Air

- *Light:* Full sun preferred, light shade tolerated for full heads, partial shade tolerated for baby leaf.
- *Air Temperature (ideal):* 60-65°F

Seed to Seedling

- *Plant Spacing After Thinning*
  - *Full Head:* 8-10 inch spacing with rows 18 inches apart <u>or</u> a uniform 12 inch spacing
  - *Baby Leaf:* 2 inch spacing in rows 5 inches apart <u>or</u> a uniform 3 inch spacing
- *Plant Spacing Before Thinning*
  - *Full Head:* No thinning necessary
  - *Baby Leaf:* 2-3 seeds per inch in rows 5 inches apart <u>or</u> a uniform 2-3 seeds every 3 inches

- *Seed Depth:* 1/4-1/2 inch
- *Days to Germination:* 3-8 days
- *Transplant or Direct Seed:* Direct seeding preferred, however transplanting is possible for full heads
- *Days from Germination to Transplanting:* 21-28 days

Harvesting

- Harvest when the plant reaches its intended size, as stated on the seed packet.
- Don't let the plant bolt (the beginning of a plant's flowering process) as this will negatively affect the plant's flavor.
- For traditional harvesting, cut the plant above the soil surface keeping the head intact. Alternatively, you can cut the leaves and stems of the plant an inch above the growing point. This will give you a loose-leaf harvest. With the growing point intact, the plant will grow new leaves and give you a second and possibly third harvest.

Storage

- Store in the refrigerator.

Tips

- If growing in light shade or partial shade, seed closer together because the plants will naturally have thinner stems and leaves due to the lack of sun.
- Plant multiple successions for a continuous harvest.

Broccoli

Brassica (brassicaceae) Family

Broccoli is cold hardy and grows moderately fast. It grows best in the cool spring and fall weather, however if you have cool summers, it may be healthy then as well. Unlike many other 'easy to grow' brassicas, broccoli can be a bit temperamental. Excessive drought or poor nutrients can cause the plant to produce a disappointingly small head. Consider growing only a couple plants to start, and then grow more the following years once you know how they perform in your garden.

High Altitude Growing Score: 5

Length of Season

- *Days to Maturity (from transplanting):* 55-75 days
- *Frost Tolerant:* Yes
- *First Direct Seeding or Transplanting:* When soil temperatures reach at least 45°F <u>or</u> 4 weeks before the last spring frost.
- *Last Transplanting:* 48-68 days before the first fall frost, depending on the variety's 'Days to Maturity'.
  - *To Calculate Last Planting:* (First fall frost date) minus (days to maturity) plus (an additional 7 days for growth after first frost)

Soil Conditions

- *Ideal pH:* 6.0-7.5
- *Soil Germination Temperature:* 50-85°F
- *Side Dressing:* 2x/season
  - *Timing:* Three weeks after transplanting, and 6 weeks after transplanting
  - *Fertilizer Type:* High nitrogen fertilizer for the first side dressing and then equal ratio N-P-K fertilizer for the second side dressing

Light and Air

- *Light:* Full sun preferred, light shade tolerated
- *Air Temperature (ideal):* 60-65°F

Seed to Seedling

- *Plant Spacing:* 12-24 inch spacing with rows 18-36 inches apart <u>or</u> a uniform 18-24 inch spacing; spacing varies greatly depending on the specific variety
- *Seed Depth:* 1/4-1/2 inch
- *Days to Germination:* 3-8 days
- *Transplant or Direct Seed:* Transplanting preferred, direct seeding is possible
- *Days from Germination to Transplanting:* 21-35 days

Harvesting

- Harvest when the head is a dark green and the buds that make up the head are just beginning to get larger and less compacted.
- To harvest, use a sharp knife and cut the stem three inches below the formed head.
- Most varieties produce one or two additional flushes of smaller side shoots of broccoli after the initial head has been harvested.
- The leaves are edible and taste similar to kale.

Storage

- Store in the refrigerator.

Tips

- Hybrid varieties tend to be much more reliable than heirloom varieties.

Brussels Sprouts

Brassica (brassicaceae) Family

Like all members of the brassica family, Brussels sprouts are cold hardy and grow well in most high altitude climates. The unique challenge with growing Brussels sprouts is accommodating their long growing season. While they are hardy enough to plant in the spring and continue growing after the first fall frost, their 'Days to Maturity' may still be too long for some garden climates.

High Altitude Growing Score: 5

Length of Season

- *Days to Maturity (from transplanting):* 80-100 days
- *Frost Tolerant:* Yes
- *First Direct Seeding or Transplanting:* When soil temperatures reach at least 45°F or 4 weeks before the last spring frost.
- *Last Transplanting:* 73-93 days before the first fall frost, depending on the variety's 'Days to Maturity'.
  - *To Calculate Last Planting:* (First fall frost date) minus (days to maturity) plus (an additional 7 days for growth after first frost)

Soil Conditions

- *Ideal pH:* 6.0-7.5
- *Soil Germination Temperature:* 45-95°F
- *Side Dressing:* 2x/season
  - *Timing:* One month after transplanting, and two months after transplanting
  - *Fertilizer Type:* High nitrogen fertilizer for the first side dressing and then equal ratio N-P-K fertilizer for the second side dressing

Light and Air

- *Light:* Full sun preferred, light shade tolerated
- *Air Temperature (ideal):* 60-65°F

Seed to Seedling

- *Plant Spacing:* 18-24 inch spacing with rows 30-36 inches apart or a uniform 24-30 inch spacing; spacing varies greatly depending on the specific variety
- *Seed Depth:* 1/4-1/2 inch
- *Days to Germination:* 3-8 days
- *Transplant or Direct Seed:* Transplanting preferred, direct seeding is possible
- *Days from Germination to Transplanting:* 21-35 days

Growing Care

- If you want all the sprouts on the plant to be ready at the same time, pinch off the plant's top growing point 4-8 weeks before the intended harvest. This stops the plant from exerting energy growing new sprouts and instead redirects the energy to the sprouts that have already begun to form.
- If you want a gradual, steady supply of sprouts from a plant, don't pinch off the growing point and instead pick them as they become firm. The lower sprouts will be ready first.
- Remove the large leaves growing near any partially formed sprouts.

Harvesting

- Pick the sprouts when they are firm. They are ready when you squeeze them and you can't feel any space in between the layers of leaves.
- The leaves are edible and can be used similarly to collards.

Storage

- Store in the refrigerator.

Cabbage

Brassica (brassicaceae) Family

Cabbage is an easy and forgiving crop to grow. It is cold hardy and grows moderately fast. Thanks to its preference for cool summers, it will many times grow better at high altitudes than in warmer sea-level climates.

Refer to page 166 for napa cabbage.

High Altitude Growing Score: 3

Length of Season

- *Days to Maturity (from transplanting):* 65-95 days
- *Frost Tolerant:* Yes
- *First Direct Seeding or Transplanting:* When soil temperatures reach at least 45°F <u>or</u> 4 weeks before the last spring frost.
- *Last Transplanting:* 58-88 days before the first fall frost, depending on the variety's 'Days to Maturity'.
  - *To Calculate Last Planting:* (First fall frost date) minus (days to maturity) plus (an additional 7 days for growth after first frost)

Soil Conditions

- *Ideal pH:* 6.0-7.5
- *Soil Germination Temperature:* 45-95°F
- *Side Dressing:* 2x/season
  - *Timing:* Three weeks after transplanting, and six weeks after transplanting
  - *Fertilizer Type:* High nitrogen fertilizer for the first side dressing and then equal ratio N-P-K fertilizer for the second side dressing

Light and Air

- *Light:* Full sun preferred, light shade tolerated
- *Air Temperature (ideal):* 60-65°F

Seed to Seedling

- *Plant Spacing:* 12-24 inch spacing with rows 24-36 inches apart <u>or</u> a uniform 18-30 inch spacing; spacing varies greatly depending on the specific variety
- *Seed Depth:* 1/4-1/2 inch
- *Days to Germination:* 3-8 days
- *Transplant or Direct Seed:* Transplanting preferred, direct seeding is possible
- *Days from Germination to Transplanting:* 21-35 days

Harvesting

- Harvest when the cabbage head is very firm. Frequently a cabbage head will look ready to harvest, but when you feel it, it will still feel loose from the space in between the leaves. While cabbage can be harvested at any point, if you pick it too early you are simply getting less cabbage for your work.
- Along with the cabbage head, the outer leaves of the cabbage plant are edible and tasty. Their taste and consistency is somewhere between collard greens and traditional cabbage.

Storage

- Store in the refrigerator.

Cabbage, Napa

Brassica (brassicaceae) Family

Napa cabbage grows quickly, but it is also one of the least frost tolerant plants in the brassica family. It is also easily prone to bolting in the summer heat, which means its growing season is limited to when there is no risk of frost, yet the weather is not overly hot. If you can accommodate its short growing window, it is a relatively easy crop to grow.

High Altitude Growing Score: 4

Length of Season

- *Days to Maturity (from transplanting):* 50-70 days
- *Frost Tolerant:* Yes
- *First Direct Seeding or Transplanting:* When soil temperatures reach at least 55°F <u>or</u> anytime after the last spring frost.
- *Last Transplanting:* 50-70 days before the first fall frost, depending on the variety's 'Days to Maturity'.
  - *To Calculate Last Planting:* (First fall frost date) minus (days to maturity)

Soil Conditions

- *Ideal pH:* 6.0-7.5
- *Soil Germination Temperature:* 45-95°F
- *Side Dressing:* 2x/season
  - *Timing:* Three weeks after transplanting, and six weeks after transplanting
  - *Fertilizer Type:* High nitrogen fertilizer for the first side dressing and then equal ratio N-P-K fertilizer for the second side dressing

Light and Air

- *Light:* Full sun preferred, light shade tolerated
- *Air Temperature (ideal):* 60-65°F

Seed to Seedling

- *Plant Spacing:* 12-18 inch spacing with rows 18-30 inches apart <u>or</u> a uniform 18 inch spacing
- *Seed Depth:* 1/4-1/2 inch
- *Days to Germination:* 3-8 days
- *Transplant or Direct Seed:* Either
- *Days from Germination to Transplanting:* 21-28 days

Harvesting

- Harvest when the head is full and firm. Napa cabbage never gets as firm as regular cabbage heads.

- If the plant begins to bolt, it will stop forming a firm head and should be harvested immediately. Allowing a prolonged period of bolting will negatively affect the flavor.
- Along with the cabbage head, the outer leaves of the cabbage plant are edible and tasty.

Storage

- Store in the refrigerator.

Carrots

Umbel (umbelliferae) Family

Carrots are cold hardy, moderately drought tolerant, and they are harvestable at any size, so if for whatever reason they do not grow as big as you'd like, they can still be enjoyed small. However, because of their long roots they will have a difficult time penetrating clay and rocky soils. As well, most animals will eat your carrots if they can get to them.

High Altitude Growing Score: 3

Length of Season

- *Days to Maturity (from seed):* 54-72 days
- *Frost Tolerant:* Yes
- *First Direct Seeding:* When soil temperatures reach at least 45°F <u>or</u> 3-4 weeks before the last spring frost.
- *Last Direct Seeding:* 54-72 days before the first fall frost, depending on the variety's 'Days to Maturity'.
  - *To Calculate Last Planting:* (First fall frost date) minus (days to maturity)

Soil Conditions

- *Ideal pH:* 5.5-7.0
- *Soil Germination Temperature:* 45-85°F
- *Side Dressing:* 1x/season
  - *Timing:* 6 weeks after germination
  - *Fertilizer Type:* Equal N-P-K ratio fertilizer (ex. 5-5-5)

Light and Air

- *Light:* Full sun preferred, light shade tolerated
- *Air Temperature (ideal):* 60-65°F

Seed to Seedling

- *Plant Spacing After Thinning:* 2 inch spacing with rows 12-24 inches apart <u>or</u> a uniform 3 inch spacing
- *Plant Spacing Before Thinning:* 3 seeds/inch with rows 12-24 inches apart <u>or</u> 3-4 seeds every 3 inches
- *Seed Depth:* 1/4-1/2 inch
- *Days to Germination:* 7-14 days
- *Transplant or Direct Seed:* Direct seed

Growing Care

- Plant spacing and thinning is very important with root crops. If plants are allowed to grow too close together they will not produce large roots.

- Carrots do not out-compete weeds well, and must be weeded repeatedly.

Harvesting

- Carrots can be harvested at any point when they reach their intended size.
- A pitchfork or a shovel works great for loosening the soil before pulling them up.

Storage

- Store in the refrigerator.
- Remove the leaves from the roots if storing for more than a couple of days. The leaves will continue to draw moisture and nutrients from the root, which will diminish the taste and shelf life of the root.

Tips

- If you are growing in clay or rocky soils, consider growing stouter, shallower varieties.
- Carrots have a notoriously unpredictable germination rate. It's recommended to plant significantly more seeds than are needed just in case some don't germinate well. You can always thin the plants afterwards as needed.
- Carrots have a germination period that can last two or more weeks. And when they do emerge from the soil, they are very small and can easily be missed or mistaken for a weed. If it looks like nothing is growing, be patient.

Cauliflower

Brassica (brassicaceae) Family

Cauliflower may be the most challenging plant to grow in the normally easy-to-grow brassica family. They are the least tolerant to frosts of all the brassicas, and one of the most sensitive to summer heat. Excessive heat and cold causes the plant to form small heads, if any at all. Cauliflower can be grown as a spring crop, but due to its sensitivity to summer heat, it generally grows best as a fall crop. If your season is so short that you must start growing them in the late spring/early summer for a fall harvest, consider only growing a couple of plants until you know how they grow in your climate.

High Altitude Growing Score: 6

Length of Season

- *Days to Maturity (from transplanting):* 50-95 days
- *Frost Tolerant:* Yes
- *First Direct Seeding or Transplanting:* After last spring frost.
- *Last Transplanting:* 50-95 days before the first fall frost, depending on the variety's 'Days to Maturity'.
  - *To Calculate Last Planting:* (First fall frost date) minus (days to maturity)

Soil Conditions

- *Ideal pH:* 6.0-7.5
- *Soil Germination Temperature:* 50-85°F
- *Side Dressing:* 2x/season
  - *Timing:* Three weeks after transplanting, and 6 weeks after transplanting
  - *Fertilizer Type:* High nitrogen fertilizer for the first side dressing and then equal ratio N-P-K fertilizer for the second side dressing

Light and Air

- *Light:* Full sun preferred, light shade tolerated.
- *Air Temperature (ideal):* 60-70°F

Seed to Seedling

- *Plant Spacing:* 18 inch spacing with rows 24-36 inches apart or a uniform 18-24 inch spacing
- *Seed Depth:* 1/4-1/2 inch
- *Days to Germination:* 3-8 days
- *Transplant or Direct Seed:* Transplanting preferred, direct seeding is possible
- *Days from Germination to Transplanting:* 21-35 days

Harvesting

- Harvest when the head is compact and firm, typically between 6-8

inches in diameter.
- To harvest, use a sharp knife and cut the stem below the formed head. Cauliflower will not produce side shoots like broccoli.
- The leaves are edible and taste similar to kale.

Storage

- Store in the refrigerator.

Cilantro

Umbel (umbelliferae) Family

Cilantro grows quickly and prefers cool weather. It is generally an easy crop to grow, however it does have difficulty growing in the intense summer heat, and the aromatic tender leaves are a favorite of many critters.

High Altitude Growing Score: 2

Length of Season

- *Days to Maturity (from seed):* 50-65 days
- *Frost Tolerant:* Yes
- *First Direct Seeding:* When soil temperatures reach at least 45°F <u>or</u> 2 weeks before the last spring frost.
- *Last Direct Seeding:* 50-65 days before the first fall frost, depending on the variety's 'Days to Maturity'.
  - *To Calculate Last Planting:* (First fall frost date) minus (days to maturity)

Soil Conditions

- *Ideal pH:* 6.0-7.0
- *Soil Germination Temperature:* 45-90°F
- *Side Dressing:* Not necessary

Light and Air

- *Light:* Full sun to partial shade
- *Air Temperature (ideal):* 50-70°F

Seed to Seedling

- *Plant Spacing:* 2-3 seeds/inch with rows 6-12 inches apart; no need to thin
- *Seed Depth:* 1/4-1/2 inch
- *Days to Germination:* 7-14 days
- *Transplant or Direct Seed:* Direct seed

Harvesting

- When the plant is at least 8 inches tall you can begin regularly picking the larger branches, or for one full harvest you can cut the entire plant from the root. If you harvest individual branches, still pick the entire plant before it begins to bolt, as bolting will alter the flavor of the leaves.

Storage

- Store in the refrigerator or put the sprigs in an open jar on a countertop with an inch of water, making sure that only the stem is submerged in water and not the leaves. The stems will absorb water in the same way a cut flower does in a vase.

Tips

- Cilantro grows best in cool weather. Summer heat causes premature bolting. If you are growing during the summer, consider planting in partial shade or under row cover to keep the plant cool and prevent bolting.
- Plant multiple successions for a continual harvest.

Corn, Sweet

Grass (gramineae) Family

Corn can be a challenging crop to grow in many high altitude climates. It has a long growing season and requires warm weather to germinate and grow. It grows tall with shallow roots, so it is susceptible to being blown over by heavy winds. Since it is pollinated through wind, it must be planted in relatively large blocks that may require more space than a home gardener wants to commit to corn. However, if you overcome these challenges, sweet corn, fresh from the garden is a unique and wonderful treat.

High Altitude Growing Score: 8

Length of Season

- *Days to Maturity (from seed):* 65-95 days
- *Frost Tolerant:* No
- *First Direct Seeding:* 1-3 weeks after last spring frost.
- *Last Direct Seeding:* 79-109 days before the first fall frost, depending on the variety's 'Days to Maturity'.
  - *To Calculate Last Planting:* (First fall frost date) minus (days to maturity) minus (an additional 14 days to accommodate slower growth due to cold fall weather)

Soil Conditions

- *Ideal pH:* 5.5-7.5
- *Soil Germination Temperature:* 55-95°F
- *Side Dressing:* 2x/season
  - *Timing:* When plants are 8 inches tall and again when the silks first appear
  - *Fertilizer Type:* Equal ratio N-P-K fertilizer (ex. 5-5-5)

Light and Air

- *Light:* Full Sun.
- *Air Temperature (ideal):* 60-75°F

Seed to Seedling

- *Plant Spacing:* 8-12 inch spacing with rows 30-36 inches apart
- *Seed Depth:* 1 inch
- *Days to Germination:* 5-21 days (cold temperatures cause a longer germination time)
- *Transplant or Direct Seed:* Direct seed

Harvesting

- Test corn for readiness when the silks of the corn head have partially or completely turned brown and died back, and the head feels plump and formed. To test if it's ready, carefully make a small slit in the husk and puncture one of the kernels. If clear liquid comes out then it is not ready yet, but if a white, milky liquid comes out it is ready. Corn rapidly goes from immature, to mature, to over mature, so don't wait to pick your corn.

Storage

- Store in the refrigerator.

Tips

- Each strand of silk on an ear of corn correlates to a single kernel. In order to have a head of corn where all the kernels are formed, every strand of silk must be wind pollinated. To reliably accomplish this, corn must be planted in blocks of at least 4-6 rows.
- Carefully picking an appropriate variety for your climate is always important, but especially when growing warm season crops. Choose wisely.

Cucumber

Cucurbit (cucurbitaceae) Family

Like most warm season fruiting plants, cucumbers can be challenging to grow at high altitudes. They need warm weather, consistent waterings and wild pollinators. Despite all the challenges, cucumber plants grow quickly and once they start producing fruit they can be very productive.

High Altitude Growing Score: 7

Length of Season

- *Days to Maturity (from seed):* 50-70 days
- *Frost Tolerant:* No
- *First Direct Seeding or Transplanting:* When soil temperatures reach at least 60°F <u>or</u> two weeks past the last spring frost.
- *Last Direct Seeding:* 64-84 days before the first fall frost, depending on the variety's 'Days to Maturity'. Plant earlier to allow for an extended harvest period.
  - *To Calculate Last Planting:* (First fall frost date) minus (days to maturity) minus (an additional 14 days to accommodate slower growth due to cold fall weather)

Soil Conditions

- *Ideal pH:* 5.5-7.0
- *Soil Germination Temperature:* 60-95°F
- *Side Dressing:* 2-3x/season
  - *Timing:* When plants begin to vine; again when flowers first appear; and a third time one month after flowers appear if the plant is still healthy and producing
  - *Fertilizer Type:* Equal ratio N-P-K fertilizer (ex. 5-5-5)

Light and Air

- *Light:* Full sun
- *Air Temperature (ideal):* 65-85°F

Seed to Seedling

- *Plant Spacing:*
  - *Trellised:* 12 inch spacing with rows 18 inches apart
  - *Untrellised:* 12 inch spacing with rows 48 inches apart
- *Seed Depth:* 1 inch
- *Days to Germination:* 4-10 days
- *Transplant or Direct Seed:* Direct Seeding is preferred because their roots are very fragile and do not like to be transplanted, however transplanting is possible if you are very careful

- *From Germination to Transplanting:* 28 days

Growing Care

- Trellising is not essential but it will save a lot of space in the garden.
- Cucumber plants require consistent deep waterings or they will grow at a significantly reduced speed and may not produce much fruit.
- If you are using row cover, and not growing parthenocarpic varieties or hand pollinating, be sure to remove the row cover when the plant is flowering to allow for pollinator access.

Harvesting

- For the best flavor and consistency, pick when young. A cucumber becomes bloated and rounded when overripe. When severely overripe their color gets lighter and even turn yellow.
- Cucumbers will continue producing fruit for the entire season as long as you consistently harvest them before they become overripe. Unpicked cucumbers will trigger the plant to end its fruiting stage.

Storage

- Store in the refrigerator.

Tips

- Most cucumber varieties are categorized as either pickling or slicing varieties. While this is a helpful categorization, it should not be taken too seriously. Picklers can be sliced and eaten raw, and slicers can be pickled.
- Traditional cucumber varieties require insect pollination to produce fruit. If you plan on growing cucumbers under row cover or you are in an area with a low population of pollinators, consider growing parthenocarpic varieties or hand pollinating.
- Carefully picking an appropriate variety for your climate is always important, but especially when growing warm season crops. Choose wisely.

Dill

Umbel (umbelliferae) Family

Dill is an easy crop to grow. It grows quickly and is happy in hot or cold weather. Unfortunately, the aromatic tender leaves are a favorite of many critters.

High Altitude Growing Score: 2

Length of Season

- *Days to Maturity (from seed):* 40-60
- *Frost Tolerant:* Yes
- *First Direct Seeding:* When soil temperatures reach at least 45°F <u>or</u> 2 weeks before the last spring frost.
- *Last Direct Seeding:* 40-60 days before the first fall frost, depending on the variety's 'Days to Maturity'.
  - *To Calculate Last Planting:* (First fall frost date) minus (days to maturity)

Soil Conditions

- *Ideal pH:* 5.5-6.5
- *Soil Germination Temperature:* 45-90°F
- *Side Dressing:* Not necessary

Light and Air

- *Light:* Full sun preferred, light Shade tolerated
- *Air Temperature (ideal):* 60-75°F

Seed to Seedling

- *Plant Spacing:* 2-3 seeds/inch with rows 6-12 inches apart; no need to thin
- *Seed Depth:* 1/4-1/2 inch
- *Days to Germination:* 7-14 days
- *Transplant or Direct Seed:* Direct seed

Harvesting

- When the plant is at least 8 inches tall begin regularly picking the larger branches, or for one full harvest cut the entire plant from the root. If you are harvesting individual branches you will still want to pick the entire plant before it begins to bolt, as bolting will alter the flavor of the leaves.

Storage

- Store in the refrigerator or put the sprigs in an open jar on a countertop with an inch of water, making sure that only the stem is submerged in water and not the leaves. The stems will absorb water in the same way a cut flower does in a vase.

Tips

- Plant multiple successions for a continual harvest.

Eggplant
Nightshade (solanaceae) Family

Even more than most warm weather crops, eggplants truly love the heat. This can make them a very difficult crop to grow in many high altitude climates. They will have significantly reduced fruit production if nighttime temperatures drop below 65°F for an extended period of time. If you decide to grow eggplant, make sure you grow a short season variety, plant in full sun, and consider growing them under row cover or a cloche.

High Altitude Growing Score: 10

Length of Season

- *Days to Maturity (from seed):* 50-80 days
- *Frost Tolerant:* No
- *First Transplanting:* When soil temperatures reach at least 60°F <u>or</u> 2 weeks after the last spring frost.
- *Last Direct Seeding:* 71-101 days before the first fall frost, depending on the variety's 'Days to Maturity'. Plant earlier to allow for an extended harvest period.
  - *To Calculate Last Planting:* (First fall frost date) minus (days to maturity) minus (21 days to adjust for fall's short days and cold weather)

Soil Conditions

- *Ideal pH:* 5.5-7.0
- *Soil Germination Temperature:* 60-90°F
- *Side Dressing:* 1x/season
  - *Timing:* When fruits first appear
  - *Fertilizer Type:* Equal ratio N-P-K fertilizer or high phosphorus fertilizer

Light and Air

- *Light:* Full sun
- *Air Temperature (ideal):* 70-85°F

Seed to Seedling

- *Plant Spacing:* 18 inch spacing with rows 24-36 inches apart <u>or</u> a uniform 24 inch spacing
- *Seed Depth:* 1/4 inch
- *Days to Germination:* 5-14 days
- *Transplant or Direct Seed:* Transplant
- *From Germination to Transplanting:* 42-56 days

Growing Care

- A month before the first fall frost, remove any flower blossoms to redirect all the plant's energy into ripening the current set of fruit.

Harvesting

- Harvest when the skin color is still bright and glossy. The size of the fruit when harvested depends greatly on the variety. After cutting it open, if the seeds are a dark brown than the fruit is overripe. If overripe the fruit will still be edible, but the taste and consistency will be less than ideal.

Storage

- Store in the refrigerator.

Tips

- Carefully picking an appropriate variety for your climate is always important, but especially when growing warm season crops. Choose wisely.

Garlic

Allium (Amaryllidaceae) Family

Garlic is a bit of an anomaly in the vegetable world. It is planted in the fall when most plants are being harvested, and it is harvested in the summer when most plants are still growing or just being planted. Along with its unusual growing parameters, it is very cold hardy, low maintenance, and generally undesirable to wildlife.

High Altitude Growing Score: 3

Length of Season

- *Days to Maturity (from direct seeding of clove):* 290 days (if planted in the fall and overwintered, preferred method) 90 days (if planted in the spring)
- *Frost Tolerant:* Yes
- *First Direct Seeding or Transplanting:* Within a month after the first fall frost date (for overwintering) or as soon as the soil can be worked in the spring.
- *Last Transplanting:* Due to their long growing season, generally only one planting per season.

Soil Conditions

- *Ideal pH:* 5.5-7.5
- *Side Dressing:* Not necessary

Light and Air

- *Light:* Full sun preferred, light shade tolerated
- *Air Temperature (ideal):* 55-75°F

Seed to Seedling

- *Plant Spacing:* 4-6 inch spacing with rows 12 inches apart or a uniform 6-8 inch spacing
- *Seed (Clove) Depth:* 2-3 inches deep with rounded end of the clove facing down
- *Transplant or Direct Seed:* Direct seeding of garlic clove

Hardneck vs. Softneck

- Hardneck and softneck are the two types of garlic you can grow.
  - Hardneck varieties are more cold hardy and better suited for northern climates. They produce a garlic scape (unformed flower) that must be removed, so energy can continue to be directed toward root production. The bulbs contain a single ring of cloves.
  - Softneck varieties are not as cold hardy as hardneck. They

do not produce a scape. The bulbs contain an inner and outer ring of cloves. The stalk is more pliable than hardneck varieties, and can be braided.

Growing Care

- If planting in the fall, cover the planted area with 2-4 inches of mulch to help insulate the plant through the winter. Gently rake aside the mulch in the spring as the shoots emerge from the soil.
- If growing hardneck varieties, remove the scape in the late spring/early summer. If the scape is harvested when it is 2-6 inches long, it will be edible and tasty with a mild garlic flavor.

Harvesting

- Harvest in the summer when the leaves have begun to yellow and die back. Ideal timing will be when the lower leaves have completely died and the top few leaves are mostly green but beginning to yellow.

Storage

- Garlic can be eaten immediately upon harvest, but if you want to store it for more than a week or two in the refrigerator, you will need to cure it.
- To cure, place in a shaded area with good air circulation at room temperature for 2-3 weeks. After curing, the garlic can be stored for up to a few months without needing to be refrigerated.

Tips

- Garlic planted in the fall will produce larger bulbs than when planted in the spring. Garlic can be planted in the fall in zones 4 and up (zone 3 if you heavily mulch).
- Consider saving some of the garlic cloves to use as seed for the next planting.

Kale
(and Collards)
Brassica (brassicaceae) Family

Kale is one of the easiest and most productive plants to grow in a garden, especially at high altitudes. It is frost tolerant into the 20s°F and unlike many plants that flower and go to seed in the summer heat, kale produces harvestable leaves for the entire season. There are few garden plants that are as simple and straightforward to grow as kale. They even tolerate growing in partial shade.

High Altitude Growing Score: 1

Length of Season

- *Days to Maturity (from transplanting):* 50-65 days
- *Frost Tolerant:* Yes
- *First Direct Seeding or Transplanting:* When soil temperatures reach at least 45°F <u>or</u> 4 weeks before the last spring frost.
- *Last Transplanting:* 43-58 days before the first fall frost, depending on the variety's 'Days to Maturity'. Plant earlier to get more than one leaf harvest.
    - *To Calculate Last Planting:* (First fall frost date) minus (days to maturity) plus (an additional 7 days for growth after first frost)

Soil Conditions

- *Ideal pH:* 6.0-7.5
- *Soil Germination Temperature:* 45-95°F
- *Side Dressing:* 3x/season
    - *Timing:* 1 month, 2 months and 3 months after transplanting
    - *Fertilizer Type:* High nitrogen fertilizer (ex. 5-0-0)

Light and Air

- *Light:* Full sun preferred, partial shade tolerated
- *Air Temperature (ideal):* 60-65°F

Seed to Seedling

- *Plant Spacing:* 12-18 inch spacing with rows 24 inches apart <u>or</u> a uniform 18 inch spacing
- *Seed Depth:* 1/4-1/2 inch
- *Days to Germination:* 3-8 days
- *Transplant or Direct Seed:* Transplanting preferred, direct seeding is possible
- *Days from Germination to Transplanting:* 21-28 days

Harvesting

- Harvest the lower larger leaves when their color is still vibrant and haven't begun to yellow.

Storage

- Store in the refrigerator, or put the leaves in an open jar on a countertop with two inches of water. The stems will absorb water in the same way a cut flower does in a vase.

Tips

- The leaves will get sweeter if harvested after a light frost.
- Red curly leaf varieties tend be less productive and have a tougher consistency than green curly leaf, lacinato, and red Russian varieties.
- While one plant can be harvested all season long, at some point in the season its growth will slow. Consider growing multiple successions to have a steady supply of kale all season long.

Kohlrabi

Brassica (brassicaceae) Family

Kohlrabi is a weird and fun plant to grow. It is not as cold hardy as many other brassicas, but it grows quickly and easily, and the thick skin surrounding the edible stem protects it from wildlife.

High Altitude Growing Score: 4

Length of Season

- *Days to Maturity (from transplanting):* 40-60 days
- *Frost Tolerant:* Yes
- *First Direct Seeding or Transplanting:* When soil temperatures reach at least 55°F <u>or</u> 2 weeks before the last spring frost.
- *Last Transplanting:* 40-60 days before the first fall frost, depending on the variety's 'Days to Maturity'.
  - *To Calculate Last Planting:* (First fall frost date) minus (days to maturity)

Soil Conditions

- *Ideal pH:* 6.0-7.5
- *Soil Germination Temperature:* 45-95°F
- *Side Dressing:* 1x/season
  - *Timing:* 1 month after transplanting
  - *Fertilizer Type:* Equal ratio N-P-K fertilizer (ex. 5-5-5)

Light and Air

- *Light:* Full sun preferred, light shade tolerated
- *Air Temperature (ideal):* 60-70°F

Seed to Seedling

- *Plant Spacing:* 4-6 inch spacing with rows 12-18 inches apart <u>or</u> a uniform 8 inches apart
- *Seed Depth:* 1/4-1/2 inch
- *Days to Germination:* 3-8 days
- *Transplant or Direct Seed:* Either
- *Days from Germination to Transplanting:* 21-28 days

Harvesting

- Most varieties are best harvested when the round stem is 2-4 inches in diameter, however some storage varieties are harvested up to 8 inches in diameter, so carefully read your seed packet for harvest information. If allowed to get overgrown, kohlrabi can

split and lose much of its flavor.
- The leaves of the plant can be harvested and used similar to kale.

Storage

- Store in the refrigerator.

Leeks

Allium (Amaryllidaceae) Family

Leeks are very cold hardy, and generally undesirable to animals, but they also have a very long growing season. If you are able to accommodate their long growing season, they can be an easy, low maintenance plant to grow.

High Altitude Growing Score: 5

Length of Season

- *Days to Maturity (from transplanting):* 80-120 days
- *Frost Tolerant:* Yes
- *First Direct Seeding or Transplanting:* When soil temperatures reach at least 45°F <u>or</u> 4 weeks before the last spring frost.
- *Last Transplanting:* Due to their long growing season, generally only one planting per season.

Soil Conditions

- *Ideal pH:* 6.0-7.5
- *Soil Germination Temperature:* 45-75°F
- *Side Dressing:* 3x/season
    - *Timing:* When plants are 8 inches tall, again a month after that, and again a month after that
    - *Fertilizer Type:* Equal ratio N-P-K fertilizer (ex. 5-5-5)

Light and Air

- *Light:* Full sun preferred, light shade tolerated
- *Air Temperature (ideal):* 55-75°F

Seed to Seedling

- *Plant Spacing:* 3-6 inch spacing with rows 18-24 inches apart <u>or</u> a uniform 6-8 inches apart
- *Seed Depth:* 1/4-1/2 inch
- *Days to Germination:* 7-14 days
- *Transplant or Direct Seed:* Transplanting preferred, direct seeding is possible if you have a long enough season
- *Days from Germination to Transplanting:* 21-28 days

Growing Care

- There are two ways to increase the amount of the white edible part of the leek:
    - Before planting, dig a trench 6 inches deep, and transplant into that. As the season progresses, rain will slowly erode

the trench and bury the lower parts of the plant. This will cause those buried portions of the plant to turn white and be more tender than the tough green leaves.

◦ Another option is to plant the leeks at soil level, but then 2-3 times throughout the growing season mound some of the surrounding soil around the leeks, which will bury the lower portions of the plant and cause them to turn white and tender.

Harvesting

- To ease harvest, loosen the soil with a pitch fork or shovel before pulling the leeks from the ground.

Storage

- Store in the refrigerator.

Lettuce
Aster (asteraceae) Family

Lettuce is fast growing and moderately frost tolerant. It can be grown as a full head or as loose-leaf baby leaves. It prefers to grow in cool weather and appreciates the cool summer nights frequently found at higher elevations.

High Altitude Growing Score: 2

Length of Season

- *Days to Maturity (from seed):* 28-35 (baby) 45-85 (full head)
- *Frost Tolerant:* Yes
- *First Direct Seeding or Transplanting:* When soil temperatures reach at least 50°F _or_ 2 weeks before the last spring frost.
- *Last Seeding:* 28-85 days before the first fall frost, depending on the variety's 'Days to Maturity' and if grown as a full head or baby.
    - *To Calculate Last Planting:* (First fall frost date) minus (days to maturity)

Soil Conditions

- *Ideal pH:* 6.0-7.5
- *Soil Germination Temperature:* 40-80°F
- *Side Dressing:* 1x/season
    - *Timing:* After the first harvest for baby loose leaf, or 3 weeks after germination for full head lettuce
    - *Fertilizer Type:* High nitrogen fertilizer (ex. 5-0-0)

Light and Air

- *Light:* Full sun to light shade for full heads; full sun to partial shade for baby leaf
- *Air Temperature (ideal):* 60-65°F

Seed to Seedling

- *Plant Spacing After Thinning:*
    - *Full Head:* 8-10 inch spacing with rows 12-18 inches apart _or_ a uniform 12 inch spacing
    - *Baby Leaf:* 2 inch spacing in rows 4 inches apart _or_ a uniform 3 inch spacing
- *Plant Spacing Before Thinning:*
    - *Full Head:* No thinning necessary
    - *Baby Leaf:* 3 seeds/inch in rows 4 inches apart
- *Seed Depth:* 1/4-1/2 inch
- *Days to Germination:* 4-10 days

- *Transplant or Direct Seed:* Direct seeding preferred, transplanting is possible for full heads
- *Days from Germination to Transplanting:* 14-21 days

Harvesting

- For baby leaves, harvest when the leaves are between 3-5 inches tall. Cut the plants with scissors or a knife, a half inch above the plant's growing point. With this method the plants will regrow, and you should be able to get 2-4 harvests before the plants bolt or become too tired and unhealthy to continue harvesting.
- For full heads, grow to the specified size on the seed packet making sure the plant has not begun to bolt as this causes the leaves to taste bitter. Using a knife, cut the plant below the growing point at soil level.
- To tell if a full-size lettuce head is beginning to bolt look for space on the stem between the layers of leaves. A normal head of lettuce will have very little space between these layers of leaves, but a bolting plant will. You can also feel for a pointy nub at the top of the plant where its growing point is. If you can feel the nub, it is getting ready to begin the bolting process and should be harvested.

Storage

- Store in the refrigerator.

Tips

- Plant multiple successions for a continual harvest.

Melons
(watermelon and muskmelon)
Cucurbit (cucurbitaceae) Family

Melons are very difficult to grow in cold, short season climates. They have a long growing season and need warm weather, consistent waterings, and wild pollinators. If you decide to grow melons, make sure you grow a short season variety, plant in full sun, water regularly, and consider growing them under row cover until they begin to flower (at which point pollinators need access to their flowers). Only attempt growing if you are up for the challenge.

High Altitude Growing Score: 9

Length of Season

- *Days to Maturity (from seed):* 80-110 days
- *Frost Tolerant:* No
- *First Direct Seeding or Transplanting:* When soil temperatures reach at least 60°F <u>or</u> two weeks past the last spring frost.
- *Last Direct Seeding:* 101-131 days before the first fall frost, depending on the variety's 'Days to Maturity'.
    - *To Calculate Last Planting:* (First fall frost date) minus (days to maturity) minus (an additional 21 days to accommodate slower growth due to cold fall weather)

Soil Conditions

- *Ideal pH:* 6.0-7.0
- *Soil Germination Temperature:* 60-90°F
- *Side Dressing:* 3x/season
    - *Timing:* When plants begin to vine, again when flowers first appear, and again a month after that
    - *Fertilizer Type:* Equal ratio N-P-K fertilizer (ex. 5-5-5)

Light and Air

- *Light:* Full sun
- *Air Temperature (ideal):* 70-85°F

Seed to Seedling

- *Plant Spacing:*
    - *Trellised:* 12 inch spacing with rows 18 inches apart
    - *Untrellised:* 12 inch spacing with rows 48 inches apart
- *Seed Depth:* 1 inch
- *Days to Germination:* 4-10 days
- *Transplant or Direct Seed:* Direct Seeding is preferred because their roots are very fragile and do not like to be transplanted, however transplanting is possible if you are very careful
- *From Germination to Transplanting:* 28 days

Growing Care

- Melons require consistent deep waterings, or they grow at a significantly reduced speed and do not produce much fruit.
- If you are using row cover, be sure to remove the row cover when the plant is flowering to allow for pollinator access.

Harvesting

- Different types of melons show different signs when ripe.
  - Muskmelon (commonly called cantaloupe) are ripe when the skin becomes a deeper, more vibrant color, and the fruit emits a more potent melon smell. They will easily fall off the stem when picked. If you experience resistance when picking, they may not be ripe.
  - For watermelon, to gauge ripeness, tap on the fruit wall and if it sounds hollow then it is ripe.

Storage

- Store in the refrigerator or on the countertop.

Tips

- Choose your variety very carefully. There are significant differences in the 'Days to Maturity' of different varieties.
- Melons require insect pollination to produce fruit. If you plan on growing melons under row cover, you need to remove the row cover once the plant begins to flower. After pollination, as the fruits are forming, you can put the row cover back over the plants.

Mustard and Asian Greens

Brassica (brassicaceae) Family

Common varieties include arugula, mizuna, tatsoi, and ruby streaks. They can be grown as mature cooking greens but are the best as baby greens for salads. They grow quickly and are moderately frost tolerant. They are best grown in the spring and fall, as they will frequently bolt in the summer heat.

High Altitude Growing Score: 2

Length of Season

- **Days to Maturity (from seed):** 21 days
- **Frost Tolerant:** Yes
- **First Direct Seeding or Transplanting:** When soil temperatures reach at least 45°F <u>or</u> 3 weeks before the last spring frost.
- **Last Direct Seeding:** 21 days before the first fall frost.
    - **To Calculate Last Planting:** (First fall frost date) minus (days to maturity)

Soil Conditions

- **Ideal pH:** 6.0-7.5
- **Soil Germination Temperature:** 45-95°F
- **Side Dressing:** 1x/season
    - **Timing:** After first harvest
    - **Fertilizer Type:** High nitrogen fertilizer (ex. 5-0-0)

Light and Air

- **Light:** Full sun preferred, partial shade tolerated
- **Air Temperature (ideal):** 60-65°F

Seed to Seedling

- **Plant Spacing After Thinning:** 2 inch spacing in rows 5 inches apart <u>or</u> a uniform 3 inch spacing
- **Plant Spacing Before Thinning:** 2-3 seeds per inch in rows 5 inches apart <u>or</u> a uniform 2-3 seeds every 3 inches
- **Seed Depth:** 1/4-1/2 inch
- **Days to Germination:** 3-8 days
- **Transplant or Direct Seed:** Direct seed

Harvesting

- Harvest when the leaves are between 3-6 inches tall. Cut the plant with scissors or a knife a half inch above the plant's growing point. With this method the plant will regrow and you should be able to get 2-4 harvests before the plant begins to bolt or becomes too weak or unhealthy to continue harvesting.

Storage

- Store in the refrigerator.

Tips

- If growing in light shade or partial shade, seed closer together because the plants will naturally have thinner stems and leaves due to the lack of sun.
- Plant multiple successions for a continual harvest.

Onions

Allium (Amaryllidaceae) Family

Onions are very cold hardy, and generally undesirable to critters, but they also have a very long growing season. If you can accommodate their growing season, they can be an easy, low maintenance crop to grow.

High Altitude Growing Score: 5

Length of Season

- *Days to Maturity (from transplanting):* 90-160 days
- *Frost Tolerant:* Yes
- *First Direct Seeding or Transplanting:* When soil temperatures reach at least 45°F <u>or</u> 4 weeks before the last spring frost.
- *Last Transplanting:* Due to their long growing season, generally only one planting per season.

Soil Conditions

- *Ideal pH:* 6.0-7.5
- *Soil Germination Temperature:* 45-95°F
- *Side Dressing:* 2x/season
    - *Timing:* When plants are 6 inches tall, and again when the bulbs start to form
    - *Fertilizer Type:* Equal ratio N-P-K fertilizer (ex. 5-5-5)

Light and Air

- *Light:* Full sun preferred, light shade tolerated
- *Air Temperature (ideal):* 55-75°F

Seed to Seedling

- *Plant Spacing:* Grow 3 plants together in a bunch; 6 inch spacing between bunches with rows 12-18 inches apart <u>or</u> a uniform 8 inches between bunches
- *Seed Depth:* 1/4-1/2 inch
- *Days to Germination:* 4-14 days
- *Transplant or Direct Seed:* Transplanting preferred, direct seeding is possible if you have a long enough season
- *Days from Germination to Transplanting:* 28-42 days

Harvesting

- For storage, harvest when the green tops have died back and fallen over. For fresh eating, harvest at any point once the bulbs are round and of the intended size.

Storage

- If you want to store your onions longer than a week or two in the refrigerator, you need to cure them. To do this, after picking them, let them lay in the field for a few days, rotating occasionally and covering if rainy. After a few days, cut off the dead tops of the onions and leave in a well ventilated, dry, shady area, with an ambient temperature around 75-80°F, for one month. At this point the onions are fully cured and should stay good for at least a couple more months without refrigeration.
- Sweet onions do not cure well and are best refrigerated and eaten fresh.

Parsley

Umbel (umbelliferae) Family

Parsley is cold hardy and moderately drought tolerant. Parsley is a biennial, so not only will it produce an abundant crop in its first year, but it frequently survives the winter and produces another harvest in the spring before going to seed.

High Altitude Growing Score: 3

Length of Season

- *Days to Maturity (from transplanting):* 35-50 days
- *Frost Tolerant:* Yes
- *First Transplanting:* When soil temperatures reach at least 45°F <u>or</u> 2 weeks before the last spring frost.
- *Last Transplanting:* 35-50 days before the first fall frost, depending on the variety's 'Days to Maturity'.
    - *To Calculate Last Planting:* (First fall frost date) minus (days to maturity)

Soil Conditions

- *Ideal pH:* 5.5-6.0
- *Soil Germination Temperature:* 45-85°F
- *Side Dressing:* 2x/season
    - *Timing:* One month after transplanting, and again a month after that
    - *Fertilizer Type:* High nitrogen fertilizer (ex. 5-0-0)

Light and Air

- *Light:* Full sun preferred, light shade tolerated
- *Air Temperature (ideal):* 60-65°F

Seed to Seedling

- *Plant Spacing:* 8 inch spacing with rows 12 inches apart
- *Seed Depth:* 1/4-1/2 inch
- *Days to Germination:* 21-30 days
- *Transplant or Direct Seed:* Transplanting
- *From Germination to Transplanting:* 28-35 days

Harvesting

- Pick the outer larger leaves when the plant is at least 6-8 inches tall.

Storage

- Store in the refrigerator or put the sprigs in an open jar on a countertop with an inch of water, making sure that only the stem is submerged in water and not the leaves. The stems will absorb water in the same way a cut flower does in a vase.

Tips

- Parsley is a biennial that will go to seed and then die in the spring of its second year. It can overwinter in zone 4 or higher, especially if you cover it with mulch in the fall. In the spring, once it begins going to seed, it will lose a lot of its flavor, but you should be able to get one or two good harvests before that happens.
- Soaking the seed for 24-48 hours before planting can quicken germination that can otherwise take 3-4 weeks.

Parsnips
Umbel (umbelliferae) Family

Parsnips are cold hardy, and are harvestable at any size, so if they do not grow as big as you'd like, they can still be enjoyed small. However, they also have a very long growing season, have a difficult time growing in clay and rocky soils, and are a favorite snack of many animals.

High Altitude Growing Score: 6

Length of Season

- *Days to Maturity (from seed):* 110-120 days
- *Frost Tolerant:* Yes
- *First Direct Seeding:* When soil temperatures reach at least 45°F <u>or</u> 4 weeks before the last spring frost.
- *Last Direct Seeding:* 110-120 days before the first fall frost, depending on the variety's 'Days to Maturity'.
    - *To Calculate Last Planting:* (first fall frost date) minus (days to maturity)

Soil Conditions

- *Ideal pH:* 5.5-7.0
- *Soil Germination Temperature:* 40-70°F
- *Side Dressing:* 2x/season
    - *Timing:* 6 weeks after germination, and again six weeks after that
    - *Fertilizer Type:* Equal N-P-K ratio fertilizer (ex. 5-5-5)

Light and Air

- *Light:* Full sun preferred, light shade tolerated
- *Air Temperature (ideal):* 60-65°F

Seed to Seedling

- *Plant Spacing After Thinning:* 2-3 inch spacing with rows 12-24 inches apart <u>or</u> a uniform 3-4 inch spacing
- *Plant Spacing Before Thinning:* 3 seeds/inch with rows 12-24 inches apart <u>or</u> 3-5 seeds every 3 inches
- *Seed Depth:* 1/4-1/2 inch
- *Days to Germination:* 7-21 days
- *Transplant or Direct Seed:* Direct seed

Growing Care

- Plant spacing and thinning is very important with root crops. If plants are allowed to grow too close together they will not produce

large roots.
- Parsnips do not out-compete weeds well, and must be weeded repeatedly.

Harvesting

- Parsnips can be harvested at any point when they reach their intended size.
- A pitchfork or a shovel works great for loosening the soil before pulling them up.
- One of the unique traits of parsnips is they can be overwintered in the ground and harvested in the early spring when you would normally not have much access to fresh garden produce. The root will actually be sweeter when harvested in the spring compared to the fall. If you have a lot of animals that visit you garden it may be safer to harvest them in the fall so you don't find them all eaten come spring.

Storage

- Store in the refrigerator.

Tips

- Parsnips have a very unpredictable germination rate. It's recommended to plant significantly more seeds than are needed in case some don't germinate well. You can always thin the plants afterwards as needed.
- Parsnips have a germination period that can last three or more weeks. And when they do emerge from the soil, they are very small and can easily be missed or mistaken for a weed. If it looks like nothing is growing, be patient.

Peas

Legume (fabaceae) Family

Peas are very cold hardy and are frequently the first seeds to be planted in the spring. They are quick growing and produce an abundant harvest. However, they do have a short growing window (limited to early spring) and require some form of trellising. Despite their challenges, peas are a great crop to grow at high altitudes.

High Altitude Growing Score: 4

Length of Season

- *Days to Maturity (from seed):* 58-70 days
- *Frost Tolerant:* Yes
- *First Direct Seeding or Transplanting:* When soil temperatures reach 40°F <u>or</u> 6 weeks before the last spring frost <u>or</u> as soon as the soil can be worked in the spring.
- *Last Direct Seeding:* 58-70 days before the first fall frost, depending on the variety's 'Days to Maturity'. Plant earlier to allow for an extended harvest period.
    - *To Calculate Last Planting:* (First fall frost date) minus (days to maturity)

Soil Conditions

- *Ideal pH:* 6.0-7.5
- *Soil Germination Temperature:* 40-70°F
- *Side Dressing:* Not necessary

Light and Air

- *Light:* Full sun
- *Air Temperature (ideal):* 60-70°F

Seed to Seedling

- *Plant Spacing:* 2-3 inch spacing with rows 12-24 inches apart. Trellis needed for most varieties
- *Seed Depth:* 1/2-1 inch
- *Days to Germination:* 6-14 days
- *Transplant or Direct Seed:* Direct seed

Growing Care

- Trellising is needed for most varieties.

Harvesting

- Sugar snap peas are best harvested when the pods are full and rounded but before their color fades and they become hard and

dry.
- Snow peas are best harvested when they are still young and underdeveloped.
- Harvest every day, and be careful not to miss any. Peas left to mature on the vine will trigger the plant to stop producing new fruit.
- Young pea shoots and flowers are also edible and nice in a salad or stir fry.

Storage

- Store in the refrigerator.

Peppers
Nightshade (solanaceae) Family

Peppers are a challenging crop to grow at high altitudes. They grow slowly, love heat, need full sun, and frequent waterings. If you decide to grow peppers, make sure to grow a short season variety, and strongly consider growing them under row cover or a cloche.

High Altitude Growing Score: 9

Length of Season

- *Days to Maturity (from transplanting):* 60-90 days, longer for some hot pepper varieties
- *Frost Tolerant:* No
- *First Transplanting:* When soil temperatures reach at least 55°F <u>or</u> 2 weeks after the last spring frost.
- *Last Transplanting:* 81-111 days before the first fall frost, depending on the variety's 'Days to Maturity'. Plant earlier to allow for an extended harvest period.
  - *To Calculate Last Planting:* (First fall frost date) minus (days to maturity) minus (21 days to adjust for fall's short days and cold weather)

Soil Conditions

- *Ideal pH:* 5.5-7.0
- *Soil Germination Temperature:* 60-90°F
- *Side Dressing:* 2x/season
  - *Timing:* One month after transplanting, and again a month after that
  - *Fertilizer Type:* Equal ratio N-P-K fertilizer (ex. 5-5-5)

Light and Air

- *Light:* Full sun
- *Air Temperature (ideal):* 70-85°F

Seed to Seedling

- *Plant Spacing:* 12-18 inch spacing with rows 24-36 inches apart <u>or</u> a uniform 18-24 inch spacing
- *Seed Depth:* 1/4 inch
- *Days to Germination:* 6-12 days
- *Transplant or Direct Seed:* Transplant
- *From Germination to Transplanting:* 42-56 days

Harvesting

- Peppers can be harvested when ripe (yellow, orange, red) or when unripe (green).

Storage

- Store in the refrigerator.

Tips

- Hot peppers are less likely to be eaten by animals than sweet varieties.
- Carefully picking an appropriate variety for your climate is always important, but especially when growing warm season crops. Choose wisely.

Perennial Herbs

Chives, Oregano, Thyme, Sage, Mint, Rosemary, Lavender
Various Families

Perennial herbs can be slow growing at first, but once established they are generally low maintenance and productive. When most of your vegetables are replanted every year, it can be a real treat to have a perennial herb area that comes back on its own every spring.

High Altitude Growing Score: 3

Length of Season

- *Perennial Hardiness*
  - *Chives:* Zone 3
  - *Oregano:* Zone 4
  - *Thyme:* Zone 5
  - *Sage:* Zone 4
  - *Mint:* Zone 4
  - *Rosemary:* Zone 6
  - *Lavender:* Zone 5
- *Days to Maturity (from transplant):*
  - *Chives:* 40-60 days
  - *Oregano:* 80-90 days
  - *Thyme:* 90-95 days
  - *Sage:* 80-90 days
  - *Mint:* 70-80 days
  - *Rosemary:* 90-120 days
  - *Lavender:* 100-110 days
- *Frost Tolerant:* Yes
- *Transplanting Date:* Transplant after the last spring frost

Soil Conditions

- *Ideal pH:*
  - *Chives:* 5.5-7.0
  - *Oregano:* 6.5-7.5
  - *Thyme:* 5.5-7.0
  - *Sage:* 6.0-7.0
  - *Mint:* 7.0-8.0
  - *Rosemary:* 6.0-7.0
  - *Lavender:* 6.5-7.0
- *Side Dressing:* 1x/season
  - *Timing:* Once per year in the spring or fall
  - *Fertilizer Type:* Equal ratio N-P-K fertilizer or high nitrogen fertilizer

Light and Air

- *Light:*
    - ◦ *Chives:* Full sun preferred, partial shade tolerated
    - ◦ *Oregano:* Full sun preferred, light shade tolerated
    - ◦ *Thyme:* Full sun preferred, light shade tolerated
    - ◦ *Sage:* Full sun preferred, light shade tolerated
    - ◦ *Mint:* Full sun preferred, partial shade tolerated
    - ◦ *Rosemary:* Full sun preferred, light shade tolerated
    - ◦ *Lavender:* Full sun preferred, light shade tolerated
- *Air Temperature (ideal):*
    - ◦ *Chives:* 60-65°F
    - ◦ *Oregano:* 65-70°F
    - ◦ *Thyme:* 60-65°F
    - ◦ *Sage:* 70-85°F
    - ◦ *Mint:* 65-70°F
    - ◦ *Rosemary:* 65-70°F
    - ◦ *Lavender:* 70-85°F

Seed to Seedling

- *Plant Spacing:*
    - ◦ *Chives:* 3-5 seedling clusters 2-8 inches apart in rows 18 inches apart
    - ◦ *Oregano:* 12-18 inch spacing
    - ◦ *Thyme:* 6-8 inch spacing in rows 12-18 inches apart <u>or</u> a uniform 10 inch spacing
    - ◦ *Sage:* 12-18 inch spacing
    - ◦ *Mint:* 12-18 inch spacing
    - ◦ *Rosemary:* 24 inch spacing
    - ◦ *Lavender:* 12-18 inch spacing in rows 24-36 inches apart
- *Seed Depth:*
    - ◦ *Chives:* 1/4 inch
    - ◦ *Oregano:* On soil surface, seed requires light to germinate
    - ◦ *Thyme:* On soil surface, seed requires light to germinate
    - ◦ *Sage:* 1/4 inch

- ◦ *Mint:* On soil surface, seed requires light to germinate
  - ◦ *Rosemary:* Lightly cover, seed requires some light to germinate
  - ◦ *Lavender:* Lightly cover, seed requires some light to germinate
- *Days to Germination:*
  - ◦ *Chives:* 7-14
  - ◦ *Oregano:* 7-21
  - ◦ *Thyme:* 14-28
  - ◦ *Sage:* 7-21
  - ◦ *Mint:* 7-14
  - ◦ *Rosemary:* 14-28
  - ◦ *Lavender:* 14-28
- *Transplant or Direct Seed:* Transplant
- *Days from Germination to Transplanting:*
  - ◦ *Chives:* 35-50
  - ◦ *Oregano:* 42-56
  - ◦ *Thyme:* 42-56
  - ◦ *Sage:* 35-50
  - ◦ *Mint:* 35-50
  - ◦ *Rosemary:* 42-56
  - ◦ *Lavender:* 42-56

Harvesting

- Harvest when the plants are full and bushy. Harvest by cutting thyme, sage, mint, lavender, and rosemary down to 6-8 inches, oregano down to 3 inches, and chives down to 1 inch.
- Many perennial herbs, especially mint, thyme, chives, and oregano slow down leaf production once they have successfully gone to seed. To have a continual supply of herbs throughout the entire growing season, harvest the plants before they flower and produce seeds. Even if you don't intend to utilize the harvested herbs, you should still trim back the plant before it can produce flowers, so later in the season it will still produce the edible leaves when you want them.

Storage

- Store in the refrigerator or put the sprigs in an open jar on a countertop with an inch of water, making sure that only the stem is submerged in water and not the leaves. The stems will absorb water in the same way a cut flower does in a vase.

Tips

- Rosemary and lavender may not survive through the winter in many high altitude climates. However, they grow excellently in pots kept outside in the spring through fall, and brought inside for the winter.

Potatoes

Nightshade (solanaceae) Family

Despite potatoes being tender to frost, potatoes are relatively easy to grow in areas with a short, cold growing season. In fact, since most of their initial growth is underground, they can be planted two weeks before the last spring frost. And if you utilize the greensprouting technique (discussed below), you can shorten the growing season by another two weeks. While potatoes still require a relatively long growing season, consistent watering, and well-drained soil, they are by far the easiest nightshade crop to grow at high altitudes.

High Altitude Growing Score: 5

Length of Season

- *Days to Maturity (from root cutting):* 90-120
- *Frost Tolerant:* No
- *First Planting:* Two weeks before the last spring frost.
- *Last Planting:* 90-120 days before the first fall frost, depending on the variety's 'Days to Maturity'.
  - *To Calculate Last Planting:* (First fall frost date) minus (days to maturity)

Soil Conditions

- *Ideal pH:* 5.0-6.5
- *Soil Sprouting Temperature:* 45-60°F
- *Side Dressing:* 1x/season
  - *Timing:* One month after plants emerge from the soil
  - *Fertilizer Type:* Equal ratio N-P-K fertilizer (ex. 5-5-5)

Light and Air

- *Light:* Full sun preferred, light shade tolerated
- *Air Temperature (ideal):* 60-65°F

Seed to Seedling

- *Plant Spacing:* 8-12 inch spacing with rows 24-36 inches apart
- *Seed Depth:* 2-3 inches
- *Days to Germination:* 5-14 days
- *Transplant or Direct Seed:* Transplant 2-inch pieces of a potato that have 1-2 eyes (small indents in the potato, where the new potato plants will grow from)

Greensprouting

Greensprouting is a technique where you let the seed potatoes develop sprouts before planting. Greensprouting gives you a two-week head start on the growing season.

1. Place whole, uncut potatoes into a ventilated box or crate, and place in a high humidity environment with normal lighting. A

greenhouse is ideal for this, but any room in a house will also work. Keep them dry to prevent rotting. Leave them for two weeks until 1/8 inch sprouts form.

2. Move the box or crate to a cool area, around 50°F, with normal lighting. A well-lit unheated basement works well. The sprouts will grow to 1/4-1/2 inch. The potatoes are now fully sprouted.

3. Cut the seed potatoes into roughly 2 inch pieces that have 1-2 sprouts on them.

4. Plant.

Growing Care

- Potatoes grow best when portions of the above ground plant are regularly buried throughout the season. This encourages new root and potato growth. To do this:
  - Before planting, dig a 6-8 inch trench and plant potatoes into it.
  - 3-4 times throughout the season, cover the new growth with soil from in between the planted rows until the plants are no longer in a trench but instead are growing on 8-12 inch hills.

Harvesting

- For young potatoes, dig up plants as early as 7-8 weeks after planting.
- For regular potatoes, wait until the fall when the plant's leaves naturally die back. Wait another two weeks from this point for the potato skins to harden underground before digging them up.

Storage

- Store in a dark, room temperature area like a cupboard, or in a paper bag on the counter.

Radishes, Spring
Brassica (brassicaceae) Family

Spring radishes are one of the fastest growing vegetables (21-28 days). They are cold hardy and are grown early in the spring and late into the fall. Because of their spiciness, most animals avoid them. They are prone to bolting in intense heat, so they should primarily be grown in the spring and fall, and only grown in the summer if you live in an especially cold climate.

High Altitude Growing Score: 3

Length of Season

- *Days to Maturity (from seed):* 21-28 days
- *Frost Tolerant:* Yes
- *First Direct Seeding:* When soil temperatures reach at least 45°F <u>or</u> 3-4 weeks before the last spring frost.
- *Last Direct Seeding:* 21-28 days before the first fall frost.
  - *To Calculate Last Planting:* (First fall frost date) minus (days to maturity)

Soil Conditions

- *Ideal pH:* 6.0-7.5
- *Soil Germination Temperature:* 45-90°F
- *Side Dressing:* Not necessary

Light and Air

- *Light:* Full sun preferred, light shade tolerated
- *Air Temperature (ideal):* 60-65°F

Seed to Seedling

- *Plant Spacing After Thinning:* 1-2 inch spacing in rows 8-10 inches apart <u>or</u> a uniform 3 inch spacing
- *Plant Spacing Before Thinning:* 2 seeds per inch in rows 8-10 inches apart <u>or</u> a uniform 2-3 seeds every 3 inches
- *Seed Depth:* 1/4-1/2 inch
- *Days to Germination:* 3-8 days
- *Transplant or Direct Seed:* Direct seed

Growing Care

- Plant spacing and thinning is very important with root crops. If plants are allowed to grow too close together they will not produce large roots.

Harvesting

- Harvest when the root is round, bright, and has not started to bolt.

- You can tell the radish is beginning to bolt by looking at the space on the stem between the layers of leaves. A non-bolting radish will not have any space between the leaves while a bolting radish will.
- Radishes are at their ideal size and flavor for only a couple days, so don't wait to pick.
- The leaves are edible, although they are best cooked, and are more bitter than most brassica leaves.

Storage

- Store in the refrigerator.
- Remove the leaves from the roots if storing for more than a couple of days. The leaves will continue to draw moisture and nutrients from the root, which will diminish the taste and shelf life of the root.

Tips

- Radishes are very sensitive to warm weather and will bolt prematurely in the heat. Only grow when the daytime temperatures are below 80°F.
- Plant multiple successions for a continual harvest.

Radishes, Rutabagas and Turnips
Brassica (brassicaceae) Family

This group of brassicas all have similar growing parameters and make excellent high altitude crops. They grow fast, prefer cool weather, and their natural spiciness will frequently deter wildlife.

High Altitude Growing Score: 3

Length of Season

- *Days to Maturity (from seed)*
  - *Daikon Radish:* 45-60 days
  - *Large Radishes:* 45-55 days
  - *Traditional Turnips:* 35-60 days
  - *Spring Salad Turnips:* 35-45 days
  - *Rutabagas:* 65-95 days
- *Frost Tolerant:* Yes
- *First Direct Seeding:* When soil temperatures reach at least 45°F <u>or</u> 4 weeks before the last spring frost, except for daikon radishes which prefer to be planted in the early summer for a fall harvest.
- *Last Direct Seeding:* 35-95 days before the first fall frost, depending on the variety's 'Days to Maturity'.
  - *To Calculate Last Planting:* (First fall frost date) minus (days to maturity)

Soil Conditions

- *Ideal pH:* 6.0-7.5
- *Soil Germination Temperature:* 45-90°F
- *Side Dressing:* 1x/season
  - *Timing:* One month after seeding
  - *Fertilizer Type:* Equal ratio N-P-K fertilizer (ex. 5-5-5)

Light and Air

- *Light:* Full sun preferred, light shade tolerated
- *Air Temperature (ideal):* 60-65°F

Seed to Seedling

- *Plant Spacing After Thinning:*
  - *Daikon Radish:* 4-6 inch spacing with rows 12-18 inches apart
  - *Large Radishes:* 2-3 inch spacing with rows 12 inches apart
  - *Traditional Turnips:* 2-3 inch spacing with rows 12-18 inches apart

- *Spring Salad Turnips:* 2-3 inch spacing with rows 12 inches apart
  - *Rutabagas:* 6 inch spacing with rows 18-24 inches apart
- *Plant Spacing Before Thinning:*
  - *Daikon Radish:* 1 seed/inch with rows 12-18 inches apart
  - *Large Radishes:* 1 seed/inch with rows 12 inches apart
  - *Traditional Turnips:* 1 seed/inch with rows 12-18 inches apart
  - *Spring Salad Turnips:* 1 seed/inch with rows 12 inches apart
  - *Rutabagas:* 3 seeds every 6 inches with rows 18-24 inches apart
- *Seed Depth:* 1/4-1/2 inch
- *Days to Germination:* 3-8 days
- *Transplant or Direct Seed:* Direct seed

Growing Care

- Plant spacing and thinning is very important with root crops. If plants are allowed to grow too close together they will not produce large roots.

Harvesting

- Harvest when the root reaches its intended size (as stated on the seed packet) but before bolting.
- You can tell the plant is beginning to bolt by looking at the space on the stem between the layers of leaves. A non-bolting plant will not have any space between the leaves while a bolting plant will.
- The leaves are edible.

Storage

- Store in the refrigerator.
- Remove the leaves from the roots if storing for more than a couple of days. The leaves will continue to draw moisture and nutrients from the root, which will diminish the taste and shelf life of the root.

Tips

- These plants are very sensitive to warm weather. Unless your summers stay cool, these plants are best grown in the spring and fall. Daikon radishes are the exception to this, since they prefer to be planted in the summer for a fall harvest.

Spinach
Goosefoot (chenopodiaceae) Family

Spinach thrives in cold weather. Seed it in the garden as soon as the soil can be worked. Its main drawback is its sensitivity to the summer heat, which can cause premature bolting. If you grow spinach only in the spring and fall, it is an easy and forgiving crop to grow.

High Altitude Growing Score: 3

Length of Season

- *Days to Maturity (from seed):* 28-52 days
- *Frost Tolerant:* Yes
- *First Direct Seeding or Transplanting:* When soil temperatures reach at least 45°F <u>or</u> 4-6 weeks before the last spring frost.
- *Last Direct Seeding:* 21-45 days before the first fall frost, depending on the variety's 'Days to Maturity'. Plant earlier to get more than one leaf harvest.
    - *To Calculate Last Planting:* (First fall frost date) minus (days to maturity) plus (an additional 7 days for growth after first frost)

Soil Conditions

- *Ideal pH:* 6.0-7.5
- *Soil Germination Temperature:* 45-75°F
- *Side Dressing:* 1x/season
    - *Timing:* One month after transplanting
    - *Fertilizer Type:* High nitrogen fertilizer (ex. 5-0-0)

Light and Air

- *Light:* Full sun to light shade preferred, partial shade tolerated
- *Air Temperature (ideal):* 60-65°F

Seed to Seedling

- *Plant Spacing After Thinning:* 2-3 inch spacing with rows 6-10 inches apart
- *Plant Spacing Before Thinning:* 2-3 seeds/inch with rows 6-10 inches apart
- *Seed Depth:* 1/4-1/2 inch
- *Days to Germination:* 5-14 days
- *Transplant or Direct Seed:* Direct seeding preferred, transplanting possible
- *Days from Germination to Transplanting:* 21-28 days

Harvesting

- Harvest when the largest leaves (not including the stem) are 2-4 inches long. Using a knife or scissors, cut the leaves 1/2 inch above the growing point. With this harvesting method, the plant will regrow, and you should be able to get 2-3 harvests before the plant begins to bolt or naturally becomes too tired or unhealthy to continue harvesting.
- If you let the plant get too large before harvesting, you risk it bolting, especially in hot weather.

Storage

- Store in the refrigerator.

Tips

- Spinach prefers to grow in cool weather. Grow only in the spring and fall unless your summers are especially cool.
- Spinach has a notoriously poor germination rate. Seed heavily, and then thin the plants as necessary.
- Plant multiple successions for a continual harvest.

Summer Squash and Zucchini

Cucurbit (cucurbitaceae) Family

Like most warm weather fruiting plants, summer squash and zucchini are challenging to grow at high altitudes. They need warm weather, consistent waterings and wild pollinators. Despite all the challenges, summer squash and zucchini plants do grow quickly and once they start producing fruit, they are very productive.

High Altitude Growing Score: 7

Length of Season

- *Days to Maturity (from seed):* 40-60 days
- *Frost Tolerant:* No
- *First Direct Seeding or Transplanting:* When soil temperatures reach at least 60°F <u>or</u> two weeks past the last spring frost.
- *Last Direct Seeding:* 54-74 days before the first fall frost, depending on the variety's 'Days to Maturity'. Plant earlier to allow for an extended harvest period.
  - *To Calculate Last Planting:* (First fall frost date) minus (days to maturity) minus (an additional 14 days to accommodate slower growth due to cold fall weather)

Soil Conditions

- *Ideal pH:* 6.0-7.0
- *Soil Germination Temperature:* 60-95°F
- *Side Dressing:* 2-3x/season
  - *Timing:* When plants begin to vine, again when flowers first appear, and again, if the plant is still healthy and producing, one month after flowers appear
  - *Fertilizer Type:* Equal ratio N-P-K fertilizer (ex. 5-5-5)

Light and Air

- *Light:* Full sun
- *Air Temperature (ideal):* 65-75°F

Seed to Seedling

- *Plant Spacing:* 18 inch spacing with rows 24-36 inches apart <u>or</u> a uniform 24 inch spacing
- *Seed Depth:* 1 inch
- *Days to Germination:* 4-10 days
- *Transplant or Direct Seed:* Direct seeding is preferred because their roots are very fragile and do not like to be transplanted, however transplanting is possible if you are very careful
- *From Germination to Transplanting:* 28 days

Growing Care

- Summer Squash and Zucchini require consistent deep waterings, or they grow at a significantly reduced speed and do not produce much fruit.
- If you are using row cover, and not growing parthenocarpic varieties or hand pollinating, be sure to remove the row cover when the plant is flowering to allow for pollinator access.

Harvesting

- For the best flavor and consistency, pick when the fruit is young with a light bright color. The color will darken as it gets overripe.
- Summer squash and zucchini will produce fruit for the entire season as long as you consistently harvest them before they become overripe. Unpicked fruit will trigger the plant to end its fruiting stage.

Storage

- Store in the refrigerator.

Tips

- Traditional summer squash and zucchini varieties require insect pollination to produce fruit. If you plan on growing them under row cover or you are in an area with a low population of pollinators, consider growing parthenocarpic varieties that are seedless and do not need pollination.
- Carefully picking an appropriate variety for your climate is always important, but especially when growing warm season crops. Choose wisely.

Sweet Potato

Convolvulaceae Family

The main challenge with growing sweet potatoes is their extreme sensitivity to frosts and cold weather. They have a long growing season and need temperatures no lower than 60°F. If you can accommodate these growing parameters, they are otherwise a relatively easy plant to grow.

High Altitude Growing Score: 8

Length of Season

- *Days to Maturity (from slip):* 90-125 days
- *Frost Tolerant:* No
- *First Planting:* Three weeks after the last spring frost <u>or</u> when the soil is 60°F.
- *Last Planting:* Due to their long season, only one planting per season is recommended.

Soil Conditions

- *Ideal pH:* 5.0-6.0
- *Side Dressing:* Not necessary

Light and Air

- *Light:* Full sun
- *Air Temperature (ideal):* 75-85°F

Seed to Seedling

- *Plant Spacing:* Bunches of 3-4 plants (also called slips) planted 10-18 inches apart with rows 36-60 inches apart
- *Transplant or Direct Seed:* Transplant slips

Harvesting

- Harvest right before the first fall frost by using a shovel or pitch fork to loosen the soil.

Storage

- The idea storage for sweet potatoes is at 50°F. If you don't have a place to store at that temperature, the countertop or refrigerator will work fine for a couple of weeks.

Tips

- Plants will be less healthy and grow slower in clay and rocky soils.

Swiss Chard

Goosefoot (chenopodiaceae) Family

Swiss chard is a very versatile and easy plant to grow. Like kale, it is frost tolerant and grows all through the summer without bolting. While chard is not quite as productive as kale, it is easy to grow and produces edible leaves throughout the entire growing season.

High Altitude Growing Score: 2

Length of Season

- *Days to Maturity (from seed):* 50-55 days
- *Frost Tolerant:* Yes
- *First Direct Seeding or Transplanting:* When soil temperatures reach at least 50°F <u>or</u> 2 weeks before the last spring frost.
- *Last Direct Seeding:* 50-55 days before the first fall frost, depending on the variety's 'Days to Maturity'. Plant earlier to get more than one leaf harvest.
  - *To Calculate Last Planting:* (First fall frost date) minus (days to maturity)

Soil Conditions

- *Ideal pH:* 6.0-7.0
- *Soil Germination Temperature:* 45-85°F
- *Side Dressing:* 2x/season
  - *Timing:* One month after seeding, and again a month after that
  - *Fertilizer Type:* High nitrogen fertilizer (ex. 5-0-0)

Light and Air

- *Light:* Full to light sun preferred, partial shade tolerated
- *Air Temperature (ideal):* 55-65°F

Seed to Seedling

- *Plant Spacing:* 4-6 inch spacing with rows 12-18 inches apart <u>or</u> a uniform 8 inch spacing
- *Seed Depth:* 1/4-1/2 inch
- *Days to Germination:* 5-8 days
- *Transplant or Direct Seed:* Direct seeding preferred due to its short growing season, but transplanting is possible
- *Days from Germination to Transplanting:* 28-42 days

Harvesting

- Harvest the lower larger leaves when their color is still vibrant and they haven't begun to turn yellow.

Storage

- Store in the refrigerator.

Tips

- Swiss chard can also be grown as baby greens by seeding at a density of 2 seeds per inch in rows 5 inches apart and harvesting like you would spinach.
- The white stem varieties normally grow faster and are healthier plants than the colored stem varieties.
- While one plant can be harvested all season long, at some point in the season its growth will slow. Consider growing multiple successions to have a steady supply of greens.

Tomatoes

Nightshade (solanaceae) Family

Tomatoes are challenging to grow at high altitudes, however, for many, a garden wouldn't be complete without them, which can make the challenge worthwhile. They take a long time to mature, love heat, need full sun, and require consistent waterings. If you grow tomatoes, choose your seed variety carefully and consider growing them under row cover or a cloche for at least the beginning of the season.

High Altitude Growing Score: 8

Length of Season

- *Days to Maturity (from transplanting):* 50-90 days
- *Frost Tolerant:* No
- *First Transplanting:* When soil temperatures reach at least 55°F <u>or</u> anytime after the last spring frost.
- *Last Transplanting:* 64-104 days before the first fall frost, depending on the variety's 'Days to Maturity'. Plant earlier to allow for an extended harvest period.
    - *To Calculate Last Planting:* (First fall frost date) minus (days to maturity) minus (21 days to adjust for fall's short days and cold weather)

Soil Conditions

- *Ideal pH:* 5.5-7.5
- *Soil Germination Temperature:* 50-85°F
- *Side Dressing:* 2x/season
    - *Timing:* One month after transplanting, and again a when fruits begin to appear
    - *Fertilizer Type:* Low nitrogen fertilizer

Light and Air

- *Light:* Full sun
- *Air Temperature (ideal):* 70-75°F

Seed to Seedling

- *Plant Spacing:* 18-36 inch spacing
- *Seed Depth:* 1/4 inch
- *Days to Germination:* 7-14 days
- *Transplant or Direct Seed:* Transplant
- *From Germination to Transplanting:* 42-70 days

Determinate vs. Indeterminate

- Determinate tomatoes are plants that have a distinct vegetative growth phase and a separate fruiting phase. These plants will grow to a certain size and then produce all their fruit at once. Determinate plants are shorter, sometimes not even needing trellising. They also tend to have a shorter 'Days to Maturity' than indeterminate tomatoes and therefore are a great choice for short season climates. Traditionally, determinate tomatoes were bred to be mostly paste varieties, so people would have a large flush of paste tomatoes all at once for canning. Nowadays, there is a relatively good selection of slicing and cherry tomatoes that are determinate.

- Indeterminate tomatoes are plants that continue producing vegetative growth even after they begin their fruiting phase. They slowly and continually produce small amounts of ripe fruit throughout the season. Most of the best tasting and prolific tomato varieties are indeterminate. However, they also take a long time to grow and generally need trellising.

Growing Care

- Trellising is needed for most varieties.

Harvesting

- For the richest flavor, pick tomatoes when fully ripe. While the flavor won't be as great, you can also pick them at any point after they have begun to ripen and let them finish ripening inside.

Storage

- Store on the countertop. Only put in the refrigerator if the tomato is fully ripe. Storing an unripe tomato in the refrigerator will diminish the flavor.

Tips

- Tomatoes are unique in that their main stem will produce roots if buried underground. When transplanting, remove the bottom half of the leaves and bury the plant up to that leafless point. This helps the plant develop a vigorous root system.
- If the first fall frost is due and there are unripe tomatoes on the vine, you can still pick them as they may ripen off of the vine. If they don't seem to be ripening, you can fry or pickle them as green tomatoes.
- Carefully picking an appropriate variety for your climate is always important, but especially when growing warm season crops. Choose wisely.

Winter Squash

Cucurbit (cucurbitaceae) Family

Like most warm season fruiting plants, winter squash is challenging to grow at high altitudes. They have a long growing season, and need warm weather, consistent waterings, and wild pollinators. Before seeding, make sure you have enough time before the first fall frost for the plant to reach maturity.

High Altitude Growing Score: 9

Length of Season

- *Days to Maturity (from seed):* 70-110 days
- *Frost Tolerant:* No
- *First Direct Seeding or Transplanting:* When soil temperatures reach at least 60°F <u>or</u> two weeks past the last spring frost.
- *Last Planting:* 84-124 days before the first fall frost, depending on the variety's 'Days to Maturity'.
  - *To Calculate Last Planting:* (First fall frost date) minus (days to maturity) minus (an additional 14 days to accommodate slower growth due to cold fall weather)

Soil Conditions

- *Ideal pH:* 6.0-7.5
- *Soil Germination Temperature:* 60-95°F
- *Side Dressing:* 2x/season
  - *Timing:* When plants begin to vine, and again when flowers first appear
  - *Fertilizer Type:* Equal ratio N-P-K fertilizer (ex. 5-5-5)

Light and Air

- *Light:* Full sun
- *Air Temperature (ideal):* 65-75°F

Seed to Seedling

- *Plant Spacing:* 18-48 inch spacing with rows 72 inches apart (spacing varies greatly based on variety)
- *Seed Depth:* 1 inch
- *Days to Germination:* 4-10 days
- *Transplant or Direct Seed:* Direct seeding is preferred because their roots are very fragile and do not like to be transplanted, however transplanting is possible if you are very careful
- *From Germination to Transplanting:* 28 days

Growing Care

- Winter squash requires consistent deep waterings or they will grow at a significantly reduced speed and will not produce much fruit.
- If you are using row cover be sure to remove it when the plant is flowering to allow for pollinator access.

Harvesting

- Harvest when the squashes are a deep color and the skin is hard. It is fine to harvest after a light frost even though it may damage or kill the leaves, but it is important to harvest before a hard frost as that could damage the fruit.

Storage

- Store on the countertop.

Tips

- Carefully picking an appropriate variety for your climate is always important, but especially when growing warm season crops. Choose wisely.

Appendix 1

Row Cover

Row cover is a thin white fabric designed to be draped over a specific plant or an entire bed, in order to keep it warm, retain moisture, keep away animals, pests and disease, and ease transplanted veggies to the shock of the high altitude sun. It is thin enough to let sunlight and water through, yet thick enough to help your plants in a myriad of ways.

Hoops or No Hoops

Row cover can be placed directly over your crops or you can place arched semicirclular hoops underneath the row cover to prop it up, so it is not directly touching the plants beneath it. In most situations, adding these hoops is not necessary.

The only time it may be worthwhile to have the row cover resting on hoops rather than the plants is when you're using the row cover to protect against a frost. Many times on a freezing night, the row cover will freeze along with anything the it is directly touching, however the air beneath the row cover will stay above freezing. This means that if the row cover is resting on a leaf, that leaf will freeze and be damaged, even though the rest of the plant will be fine. Whether or not this is a problem is entirely dependent on the plant you're growing. If a couple tomato leaves receive a little frost damage, that won't significantly affect the plant's health, however if a lettuce leaf gets frost damage, that is a problem since you were planning on eventually eating that leaf. In a situation where you're providing frost protection to a plant that you eat the leaves of, it is a good idea to add hoops.

If you choose to use hoops you can make them by bending PVC, metal conduit, or any type of metal (such as from an old clothes hanger) into an arch and securing it into the soil on either side of the garden bed. Depending on what you use to make the hoops, they may not be sturdy enough to support the row cover in the event of a serious snow storm, however they will still work well in most situations.

The distance in between hoops should range from 3-10 feet. Place them at whatever distance works to keep the row cover from touching the plants.

Securing Row Cover to the Ground

Whether using hoops or not, an important factor to consider is how you will secure the row cover to the ground. If the row cover is not properly weighed down it has a tendency to catch the wind like a sail and may never be seen again. You can use rocks, sandbags, or shovel a bit of dirt onto its edges to weigh it down. What you use as a weight is not as important as how much weight you use. Try to use weights that are 10-15 pounds and place them every 3-10 feet depending on how windy your area is. Remember, you will regularly remove the row cover to weed, harvest, and admire your plants, so find that balance of it being secured to the ground, yet not too difficult to remove.

Types of Row Cover

There are different row cover thicknesses to choose from. The thickest ones are intended for frost protection while the thinnest ones are intended for pest protection. While some thicknesses are better suited for specific tasks, they all work. The drawback of the thickest row cover is it blocks more sunlight than the thinner ones. And the drawback of the thinnest row cover, along with it providing less frost protection, is it is more prone to ripping. If you're going to purchase only one type, my recommendation is to get a medium thickness row cover, since it will work well enough for all your row cover needs.

If you don't have row cover, or don't have enough, you

can also use a bed sheet. The drawback of a sheet is that it will not let light and water through, so it is best suited as a last resort when covering plants through the night during a frost warning. If needed, you can leave the sheet over a plant for a couple of days without much damage, but any longer than that and the plants will suffer.

Appendix 2

Raised Beds

There are many ways to make a raised bed. It can be as simple as adding a bit of soil or compost to a regular garden bed, so it is raised an inch or two above the rest of the soil, or you can construct a raised bed to be four-feet above the ground, so you never have to kneel or lean over. There is no wrong way to make a raised bed and the design you choose depends entirely on your preferences. If you want a simple wood-framed raised bed that will warm up faster in the spring, help with soil drainage, and looks nice, the below design might be right for you.

Simple 10-Inch High Rectangular Raised Bed

Material

- 2in x 10in redwood or cedar planks, cut to the dimensions of your rectangular bed
- (8) 3-inch decking screws, (8) 3-inch decking nails, or outdoor wood glue– to secure the four 2in x 10in planks to each other
- (8) 2-3 foot pieces of rebar
- (16) 1/2 inch conduit clamps
- (32) 1.5 inch decking screws
- Soil

Instructions

1. Cut the wooden planks to the desired bed dimensions.
2. Screw, nail, or glue the wooden planks together to form a rectangle.
3. Place the rectangular bed exactly where you want it to permanently stay.
4. Using a hammer, pound the rebar into the soil on the inside of the rectangular bed, flush with the wooden planks (two pieces of rebar for each wall of the bed).

Pound the rebar so only 8 inches of it is above the soil.

5. Using the conduit clamps and the 1.5 inch decking screws (2 clamps per rebar), attach the rebar to the wooden frame.

6. Fill the bed with top soil, potting mix or a topsoil/compost mix.

Variations

- Redwood and cedar are very expensive woods, but they are rot resistant and last outdoors for many years without needing to be replaced. However, if you want to use a different wood you can treat it with linseed oil to prevent it from rotting. You can also line the inside of the bed walls with plastic sheeting to protect it from rotting. If you use a plastic lining, be sure to only cover the walls and not the ground. If the ground is covered in plastic then water will not be able to drain out of the bed. Also, don't use pressure treated wood or toxic weather-proofing paints, as these are harmful to plants.

- If you are concerned about burrowing animals, you can line the bottom of the bed with 1/2 inch metal hardware cloth and use staples, nails or screws to attach it to the bottom of the wood frame.

Appendix 3

Weed Mat

Weed mat is a tarp-like fabric that is secured to the surface of a garden bed, so plants can then be planted into it through strategically placed holes. It is used primarily as a weed suppressant/barrier but is also great at warming the soil and keeping it from prematurely drying out.

The setup involved with weed mat is fairly intensive, but once in place, a good quality woven weed mat can last ten or more years outside in the elements. Because of its setup it is best suited for permanent beds that do not need to be re-tilled every year, however if you're motivated you can temporarily remove it every year to prep the area for the next year's crops

Installing Weed Mat

1. After prepping the soil for planting, cover the entire bed with the mat. It's helpful to leave roughly four inches of extra mat extending past the perimeter of the bed for when you secure the mat to the ground in step two. You can use multiple small pieces to cover a bed, just make sure they are properly overlapping; weeds love finding ways to grow through little cracks.

2. Secure the mat to the ground. This is easily done with landscaping staples, which can be bought online or at your local nursery. If you don't have landscaping staples, you can bury the edges of the weed mat in a trench or use rocks or sandbags to hold it in place.

3. Create holes in the mat to transplant or seed the plants through. At this point you need to know what you're planting, so you can space the holes accordingly. For example, if you're planning on growing kale in a bed you will want a hole every 12 inches, whereas if you're growing tomatoes, you'll want the holes every 18 inches. Cut a 2-3 inch diameter hole using scissors or a sharp

serrated knife. This fabric has a tendency to fray or rip over time so if you're inclined you can lightly singe the edges of the circle with a lighter, so it won't fray.
4. Plant! Direct seeding and transplanting both work great with this method.

Hole Spacings

Over the years you may want to grow crops of different spacings. You can accomplish this by having holes every six inches. With holes every six inches you can do 6,12,18 and 24-inch plant spacings, which will accommodate many vegetables. However, the downside to this is that having extra unused holes in your weed mat encourages some weed growth.

Weed mat works best with crops that require a spacing of at least six inches. Any closer than six inches and you end up creating so many holes in the fabric that it defeats the purpose. This means that certain crops like loose leaf salad greens or carrots will not grow well with weed mat.

Adding Mulch

If you don't like the look of the weed mat, you can cover it with mulch to give it more of a natural look. Any type of mulch will work, such as wood chips, straw, or hay.

Appendix 4

Mulch

Mulch is a great way to stop weeds and retain moisture in the soil. It significantly reduces the amount of time you spend weeding, and the amount of water you use. Mulch can be any organic material that you place on the surface of your garden bed or in the aisles in between the beds. Another benefit of mulch is after it has decomposed, it adds organic matter back into the soil. The most common examples of mulch are hay, straw, wood chips and dead leaves.

Types of Mulch

Frequently the best mulch to use is the one you have readily available. If you have a lot of wood chips or dried leaves from landscaping projects, use those. If your neighbor sells hay, use that. There are however slight differences in how mulch functions in your garden and how long it lasts before needing to be   replaced.

- *Hay:* Hay is predominantly tall grass that has been mowed, dried and baled. It is an easy and affordable mulch option, however many times hay has weed seeds in it. If you use hay, be sure to weed if necessary. Hay needs to be replaced every year once it has decomposed.

- *Straw:* Straw are the dried stalks of cereal crops, such as wheat, barley or rye. Because the cereal grains, which are the seeds of the plant, have been harvested prior to being baled and sold as straw, there should not be any seeds left. For this reason, if you have a choice between hay and straw, choose straw. Straw needs to be replaced every year once it has decomposed.

- *Wood Chips:* Wood chips are heavier than many

mulches, therefore if you are in a windy area they are a good choice. They also take much longer than most other mulches to decompose, so you can go longer in between reapplying. Unfortunately, wood chips tend to rob nutrients from the soil as they decompose. However, this will only be an issue if they get buried under the soil. Therefore, instead of using them on seasonally tilled annual garden beds, where they will likely get buried at the end of the season, consider using them for no-till beds, perennial beds, or for the aisles in between beds. Wood chips need to be replaced every 3-4 years once they have decomposed.

- *Dead Leaves:* Depending on your area and the trees on your property, you may be fortunate enough to have a large supply of free leaves. Leaves make great mulch, however they are very light and therefore prone to blowing away. Leaves need to be replaced every year once they have decomposed.

Amount of Mulch

Whatever type of mulch you use, you want to apply a thick layer, generally at least 3 inches. While a light layer of mulch may still look nice, it won't stop weeds and will only minimally help retain water in the soil.

Glossary

- **Allium Family:** A crop family that includes onions, leeks, and garlic. Latin name: Amaryllidaceae.

- **Annual:** Garden annuals are plants that do not overwinter and will only survive for one season. Botanically, the term annual has a different meaning (see page 24). See "Perennial" and "Biennial".

- **Anther:** The part of the flower that contains the pollen. See "Stigma".

- **Apron, Fence**: A fence apron is a method for stopping burrowing animals from digging under a garden fence. It is made by burying a fence vertically at first, but then curving the fence horizontally to create an 'L' shape underground that the animals hit whenever they try to burrow.

- **Beneficial Insects**: Insects that attack pests but do not harm garden plants. Beneficial insects may be found naturally in your garden or they can be purchased.

- **Beneficial Nematodes:** Microscopic roundworms that attack certain pest populations but will not harm the host plant or other beneficial insects.

- **Biennial:** Garden biennials are plants that can survive through the winter, but will die after producing seeds in their second year. Botanically, the term biennial has a different meaning (see page 24). See "Annual" and "Perennial".

- **Bolting:** The process many plants go through when progressing from their vegetative stage to their flowering stage. For plants that produce edible leaves or roots, the bolting process will negatively affect their flavor, and those plants should be harvested prior to bolting. For many plants the first sign of bolting is a tall, elongated stem. Bolting is frequently triggered in annuals by hot temperatures.

- **Brassica Family:** A crop family that includes bok choi, broccoli, Brussels sprouts, cabbage, cauliflower, kale, kohlrabi, mustard/asian greens, napa cabbage, radish, rutabaga, and turnips. Latin name: Brassicaceae.

- **BT (Bacillus thuringiensis):** Naturally occurring beneficial bacteria you can spray on your plants and will kill a wide variety of pests.

- **Clay:** The smallest of the three particles found in soil. The largest particles are sand and the medium size particles are silt. Most soils are a mix of all three particle sizes.

- **Cloche:** A small glass or plastic covering that can go over a single plant and acts as a mini greenhouse.

- **Cold Frame:** A permanent four-walled structure that is either self-contained and filled with soil or has no floor and is placed over a garden bed. It warms up the air and soil within the frame, and allows vegetables to be planted within it up to a month earlier than the outside garden beds. It is frequently made with wooden walls and a hinged translucent lid that is slanted to face the sun. It is generally only 1 to 3 feet tall.

- **Companion Planting:** The idea that certain plants grow better or worse depending on the other types of plants in proximity to them.

- **Compost:** A source of organic matter. Compost adds organic matter and nutrients to the soil.

- **Crop Families:** Taxonomic classification for plants. Plants that are in the same family tend to have the same nutrient needs, and are susceptible to the same pests and diseases.

- **Crop Rotation:** Crop rotation is when you avoid growing the same crop family in the same place for multiple years in a row. Crop rotation is used to deter pests and diseases, as well as mitigate nutrient depletion in the soil.

- **Cross-Pollination:** Pollination that occurs using genetic material from two separate plants. See "Self-Pollination".

- **Crown:** A soil-less bare root transplant. Asparagus transplants are frequently bought this way.

- **Cucurbit Family:** A crop family that includes cucumbers, summer squash, zucchini, melons, and winter squash. Latin name: Cucurbitaceae.

- **Days to Maturity:** The number of days from direct seeding or transplanting until a plant can begin to be harvested.

- **Determinate:** A plant with determinate growth has a distinct vegetative growth phase and a separate fruiting phase. These plants will grow to a certain size and then produce all their fruit at once. See "Indeterminate".

- **Diatomaceous Earth:** The ground-up fossilized remains of small aquatic animals called diatoms. They are non-toxic to humans and other mammals but deadly to many soft-bodied pests.

- **Direct Seeding:** Planting a seed in a garden bed. The alternative to direct seeding is transplanting. See "Transplanting".

- **Disease:** Any bacteria, virus, or fungus that damages garden plants.

- **Drip Irrigation:** Lines of flexible, perforated plastic tubing placed alongside your plants and connected to a hose. Drip irrigation is the most water-efficient method for irrigating your garden.

- **Frost Tolerant:** A plant that can survive at least a light frost.

- **Fruit:** The part of the plant that contains a seed.

- **Full Shade:** An area of a garden is in full shade when it receives less than 2 hours of direct sunlight every day. See "Full Sun", "Light Shade", and "Partial Shade".

- **Full Sun:** An area of a garden is in full sun when it receives 8 or more hours of direct sunlight every day. See "Light Shade", "Partial Shade", and "Full Shade".

- **Goosefoot Family:** A crop family that includes beets, swiss chard, and spinach. Latin name: Chenopodiaceae.

- **Growing Season:** The period of time from the spring to the fall when you can grow vegetables in your garden.

- **Hardiness Zones:** Geographical areas within the United States that share a similar wintertime low temperature. These zones tell how cold-hardy a plant must be to survive in a specific area.

- **Harvest:** Gathering food from the garden.

- **Heirlooms:** Heirloom seed varieties are created by the traditional method of saving seeds from the healthiest, tastiest and most productive plants. Many heirloom varieties have been around for hundreds of years, and are a great choice if you plan to save seeds, or if you live in an unusual climate that seed companies don't breed their hybrid seeds for. Heirloom varieties, frequently, but not always, are tastier than hybrids. See "Hybrids".

- *High Altitude Growing Score:* This book's unique rating system that allows you to quickly understand the ease and suitability of growing a plant at high altitudes.

- *Hybrids:* Hybrid seed varieties are created by breeding two characteristically different varieties of a plant to make a "hybrid" variety that has the best parts of its two parents. Hybrid varieties, frequently, but not always, are healthier and more productive than heirloom varieties. Seeds should not be saved from hybrid plants, as the offspring will produce plants that have characteristics different from their parents. See "Heirlooms".

- *Imperfect Flower:* A plant flower that contains either the male or female parts (anther or stigma) but do not contain both. See "Perfect Flower".

- *Indeterminate:* A plant with indeterminate growth will continue producing vegetative growth even after they begin their fruiting phase. They slowly and continuously produce small amounts of ripe fruit throughout the season. See "Determinate".

- *Light Shade:* An area of a garden is in light shade when it receives 5 to 8 hours of direct sunlight every day. See "Full Sun", "Partial Shade", and "Full Shade".

- *Lime:* A rock powder that when added to garden soil will raise the soil's pH.

- *Low Tunnel:* A season extension technique where 3 to 4-foot-tall hoops are placed over a garden bed and then the garden bed and hoops are covered in greenhouse plastic. Low tunnels warm up the air and soil underneath the plastic, and allow vegetables to be planted up to a month earlier.

- *Mulch:* Organic material, frequently hay, straw, leaves, or wood chips, that is placed on the surface of a garden bed to help retain moisture and block weed growth.

- *Neem:* An organic spray that kills a wide range of diseases and pests.

- *Nightshade Family:* A crop family that includes tomatoes, peppers, eggplants, and potatoes. Latin name: Solanaceae.

- *Nitrogen:* One of the three most vital nutrients for plants (the other two are potassium and phosphorus). Nitrogen is the primary nutrient responsible for vegetative (leaf and stalk) growth. It is one of the main components in chlorophyll, the compound used to convert sunlight into energy for the plants.

- *No-Till:* A form of bed preparation where the soil is not aerated or disturbed before planting. No-till methods are used to avoid the eventual compaction and degradation of the soil's structure that eventually follows after tilling. See "Till" and "Sheet Mulching"

- *N-P-K:* Nitrogen-Phosphorus-Potassium are the three most vital nutrients for plants. All store-bought fertilizers have an N-P-K number listed on them that tells you what percentages of those nutrients are in the fertilizer. If a fertilizer has an N-P-K number of 5-5-5 then 5% of the fertilizer is pure nitrogen, 5% is pure phosphorus, and 5% is pure potassium.

- *Organic Matter:* Decomposed material from previously living organisms. In soil, organic matter improves soil structure, enhances water drainage, feeds beneficial microorganisms and insects, and provides nutrients to plants at a healthy rate.

- *Overwinter:* Overwintering is when a plant survives through a winter, typically in a dormant state, and continues growing into the spring.

- *Parthenocarpic:* Plant varieties that produce fruit without fertilization. Purchasing parthenocarpic seeds are necessary if you are growing plants that require insect pollination to produce fruit, yet you are growing them under row cover or in a greenhouse. The most common parthenocarpic garden vegetables are cucumbers and zucchini.

- *Partial Shade:* An area of a garden is in partial shade when it receives 2-5 hours of direct sunlight every day. See "Full Sun", "Light Shade", and "Full Shade".

- **Perennial:** Garden perennials are plants that can survive through the winter and will be alive for multiple years. Botanically, the term perennial has a different meaning (see page 24). See "Annual" and "Biennial".

- **Perfect Flower:** A plant flower that contains the male and female parts (anther and stigma) all within a single flower. See "Imperfect Flower".

- **Pest:** Any insect that damages garden plants.

- **pH:** The measure of the acidity and alkalinity in your soil. The pH scale ranges from 0-14. 14 is the most alkaline, 0 is the most acidic, and 7 is neutral.

- **Phosphorus:** One of the three most vital nutrients for plants (the other two are nitrogen and potassium). Phosphorus is the primary nutrient responsible for root development and flower production.

- **Pollination:** The transfer of pollen from the anther to the stigma that allows a plant to produce a seed and fruit.

- **Potassium:** One of the three most vital nutrients for plants (the other two are nitrogen and phosphorus). Potassium helps keep the cells within the plant strong and healthy. It also helps the plant withstand environmental stressors like extreme heat, cold and drought.

- **Pyrethrin:** An organic pesticide derived from the chrysanthemum plant.

- **Raised Bed:** A garden bed where the bed's soil is higher than the surrounding ground. The bed can be a couple of inches high, or a couple of feet. It can be contained in a frame or be a loose mound of soil.

- **Row Cover:** A thin white fabric that is designed to drape over your plants to keep them warm, retain moisture, keep away pests, and ease transplanted veggies from the shock of the high altitude sun. It is thin enough to let sunlight and water through, yet still thick enough to prevent damage from freezing temperatures.

- **Sand:** The largest of the three particles found in soil. The smallest particles are clay and the medium size particles are silt. Most soils are a mix of all three particle sizes.

- **Self-Pollination:** Pollination that occurs using only genetic material from a single plant. See "Cross-Pollination".

- **Sheet Mulching:** A no-till method of preparing a new garden bed for planting. This method involves laying cardboard over an area in the garden and then covering the cardboard with at least 3 inches of soil. Within a few months to a year, the cardboard and the weeds underneath will have decomposed and you will have a weed-free area ready for planting.

- **Sidedressing:** Applying fertilizer or compost to a plant that is already growing in the garden. While fertilizer or compost should be added to a garden bed prior to planting, many plants benefit from additional applications throughout their growing season.

- **Silt:** The medium size particles found in soil. The smallest particles are clay and the largest are sand. Most soils are a mix of all three particle sizes.

- **Soil Test:** A soil test is when you send a sample of your garden soil to a lab, and receive a soil report from them. Your soil report will tell you your garden's nutrient levels, organic matter content, and pH.

- **Stigma:** The part of the flower that pollen must come in contact with for pollination to occur. See "Anther".

- **Successions:** Growing the same type of vegetable at multiple times throughout the growing season, in order to have a longer and more continuous harvest period than if you only did one planting.

- **Thinning:** Because seeds don't always germinated it is helpful to plant multiple seeds in the same place to ensure at least one germinates. Thinning is the act of removing any extra seedlings after germination.

- **Till:** Aerating the top section of the soil to improve drainage and allow for plant roots to grow more easily through the soil. This is most commonly accomplished with a shovel, hoe, or rototiller. See "No-Till".

- *Transplanting:* Taking a plant that has been grown in a small container, in a greenhouse or on a windowsill, and planting it in the garden. Using transplants, rather than direct seeding, allows for a plant to start growing earlier in the season than it would normally be able to do outside. See "Direct Seeding".

- *Umbel Family:* A crop family that includes carrots, parsnips, cilantro, parsley, and dill. Latin name: Umbelliferae.

- *Variety:* Vegetables have many different seed varieties. Varieties of the same vegetables are genetically similar, yet are bred to express unique traits. Some varieties will be more cold tolerant, pest resistant, faster growing, or tastier than other varieties.

- *Weed Mat:* A tarp-like fabric placed on the surface of a garden bed. Holes are cut into the fabric to allow specific plants to grow through it. Weed mat is used to stop weeds, to keep soil from drying out, and to warm up the soil earlier in the spring.

- *Weeds:* A weed is any plant that you don't want in your garden, yet still manages to be there.

- *Windbreak:* A physical object placed between the wind's path and your garden. Common windbreaks include buildings, fences, bushes, and trees.

Photo Attribution

Front Cover: "Young Kale" by Leanne Korb

Chapter One

- Fig. 1: "U.S. Department of Agriculture"
- Fi g. 3: "Valley Fog" by Jay Huang is licensed under CC BY 2.0 https://www.flickr.com/photos/50663863@N02/25826507188/
- Fig. 4: Photo by USDA NRCS South Dakota is licensed under CC BY-SA 2.0 https://www.flickr.com/photos/nrcs_south_dakota/21222959783/in/album-72157668265463015/
- Fig. 7: "U.S. Department of Agriculture"

Chapter Two

- Fig. 1: "Cabbage and Frost at the Centre for Alternative Technology" by Centre for Alternative Technology is licensed under CC BY 2.0 https://www.flickr.com/photos/catimages/3098861802/
- Fig. 2: "Saving Morning Glory Seeds" by anneheathen is licensed under CC BY 2.0 https://www.flickr.com/photos/annethelibrarian/8004487635/
- Fig. 5: "United Way Day of Caring..." by Ryan is licensed under CC-ND BY 2.0 https://www.flickr.com/photos/rcferdin/9724335997/

Part Two Cover Image: "Frost Kale Leaf" by Local Food Initative is licensed under CC BY 2.0 / cropped from original https://www.flickr.com/photos/132399483@N05/31956672795/

Chapter Three

- Fig. 1: "Kurbispflanzen" by Maja Dumat is licensed under CC BY 2.0 https://www.flickr.com/photos/blumenbiene/14104294142/
- Fig. 3: "Cafe Garden" by Oor Woolie is licensed under CC BY 2.0 / cropped from original https://www.flickr.com/photos/kaskaandjim/13700265285/
- Fig. 4: "Garden Beds" by Linda N. is licensed under CC BY 2.0 https://www.flickr.com/photos/22748341@N00/1434940191/
- Fig. 5: "Portland: Spring Garden Full of Snow" by Eli Duke is licensed under CC BY-SA 2.0 https://www.flickr.com/photos/elisfanclub/6860192884/in/photostream/
- Fig. 7: "Cloches" by Mandy Prowse is licensed under CC-ND BY 2.0 https://www.flickr.com/photos/feltbug/3486857002/in/photostream/
- Fig. 8: "Beetroot" by Mandy Prowse is licensed under CC-ND BY 2.0 https://www.flickr.com/photos/feltbug/3486041443/in/photostream/
- Fig. 9: "Large Cold Frame" by Omer El-Hashahar is licensed under CC BY-SA 2.0 https://www.flickr.com/photos/best4garden/9016654476/in/photolist-yekBVr-xW3wx5-yekHgM-PSLCLr-xgMMKc-L5YFEd-25VPZKX-PSLKZp-PSLHPc-PGCwCg-PSLGXT-PSLHjK-PGCsY2-HoradR-HrvY5A-PSLG98-w2SMNN-dX4vJp-aHsYsc-6QWnPw-dQ9dUV-cdhpFo-6YjvzY-7RTFUr-bpf3qY-apda9M-e7Qeb2-Q9YVCj-bkAtvd-nJ77bn-wB2Fim-o1hyiF-o1zK24-qqQgKu-5n6W69-jEsZzw-Kenujp-Ke9RSw-BEyjgc-PogYDq-TcukCo-MsZi7D-L49PXi-Ke9PQ5-Ke9V7Y-eJLHeW-cdhLDf-5NELmT-5n6VoA-8MUdm

Chapter Four

- Fig 1: "dead patch coming to life" by Liz Henry is licensed under CC-ND BY 2.0 https://www.flickr.com/photos/lizhenry/2734302640/in/photostream/

- Fig 2: "Garden Sprinkler" by Thangaraj Kumaravel is licensed under CC BY 2.0 https://www.flickr.com/photos/kumaravel/8289465537/
- Fig. 6: "cavolo nero" by cristina.sanvito is licensed under CC BY 2.0 https://www.flickr.com/photos/40385177@N07/6008867738/

Chapter Five

- Fig. 1: "Wind-blown tree" by John Winkelman is licensed under CC BY 2.0 https://www.flickr.com/photos/johnwinkelman/6321803763/
- Fig. 2: "Peas" by Newton grafitti is licensed under CC BY 2.0 https://www.flickr.com/photos/newtown_grafitti/7850365312/

Chapter Six

- Fig. 2: "Prepping Hangar Garden for Planting -13" by Keith Rowley is licensed under CC BY-SA 2.0 https://www.flickr.com/photos/yugen/3427146133/
- Fig. 3: "Vegetable Garden, June 17" by OakleyOriginals by Keith Rowley is licensed under CC BY 2.0 / cropped from original https://www.flickr.com/photos/oakleyoriginals/20472161700/

Chapter Seven

- Fig. 1: "hpm 2011-4524.jpg" by hans peter meyer is licensed under CC BY-SA 2.0 https://www.flickr.com/photos/hanspetermeyer/6265709874/
- Fig. 6: "Compost" by U.S. Departent of Agriculture is licensed under CC BY 2.0 https://www.flickr.com/photos/usdagov/15247160284/
- Fig. 8: "Hidcote Manor Garden (NT) 10-18-2013" by Karen Roe is licensed under CC BY 2.0 https://www.flickr.com/photos/karen_roe/16149224465/

Chapter Nine

- Fig. 4: "Fence, no deer" by Deb Nystrom is licensed under CC BY 2.0 https://www.flickr.com/photos/stella12/19007612345/
- Fig. 6: "Unexpected Visitor" by Eric Kilby is licensed under CC BY-SA 2.0 https://www.flickr.com/photos/ekilby/9355982066/
- Fig. 7: "Bedtime" by Mark Gunn is licensed under CC BY 2.0 https://www.flickr.com/photos/mark-gunn/29498837687/
- Fig 9: "Bird netting in place over strawberries..." by bnpositive is licensed under CC BY-SA 2.0 https://www.flickr.com/photos/bnpositive/17702394011/
- Fig 11: "Woodchuck Houdini" by Kristin "Shoe" Shoemaker is licensed under CC-ND BY 2.0 https://www.flickr.com/photos/linuxlibrarian/7511316418/

Chapter Ten

- Fig. 3: "25 Excellent" by Lesley L. is licensed under CC BY-SA 2.0 https://www.flickr.com/photos/21932122@N02/27550274382/in/photostream/

Plant Index

- Parsnips: Photo by Sharon Mollerus is licensed under CC BY 2.0 https://www.flickr.com/photos/clairity/2445626992/
- Sweet Potatoes: "October 23, 2013. sweet potato harvest" by jalexartis Photography is licensed under CC BY 2.0 https://www.flickr.com/photos/fayncbikerjaa/10441605653/
- Winter Squash: "Squashes" by Ruth Hartnup is licensed under CC BY 2.0 https://www.flickr.com/photos/ruthanddave/426276934/

Index

CPSIA information can be obtained
at www.ICGtesting.com
Printed in the USA
BVHW050921070821
613846BV00004B/480